RICK WARREN

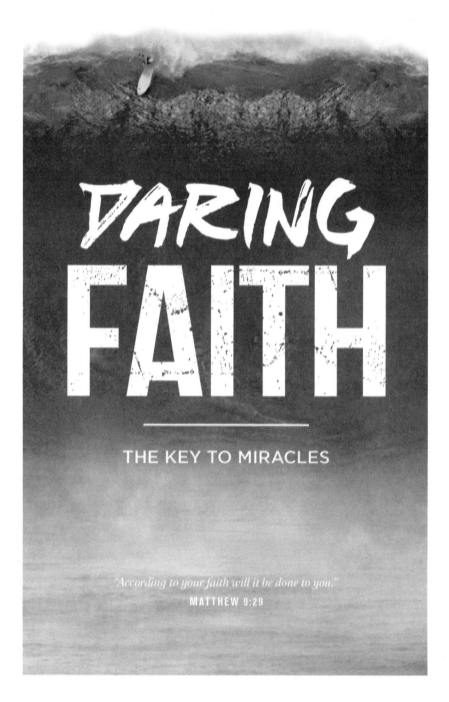

DARING FAITH

THE KEY TO MIRACLES

"According to your faith will it be done to you."

MATTHEW 9:29

DARING FAITH: THE KEY TO MIRACLES

Small Group Study Guide
Edition 2.0

Published by Purpose Driven Communications
23182 Arroyo Vista
Rancho Santa Margarita, CA 92688

Scripture quotations marked AMP are taken from the Amplified® Bible. Copyright © 1954, 1958, 1962, 1964, 1965, 1987 by The Lockman Foundation. Used by permission.

Scripture quotations marked ESV are taken from the ESV® Bible (The Holy Bible, English Standard Version®). Copyright © 2001 by Crossway, a publishing ministry of Good News Publishers. Used by permission. All rights reserved.

Scripture quotations marked GW are taken from God's Word®.Copyright © 1995 God's Word to the Nations. Used by permission of Baker Publishing Group. All rights reserved.

Scripture quotations noted HCSB are from the Holman Christian Standard Bible˚. Copyright © 1999, 2000, 2002, 2003, 2009 by Holman Bible Publishers. Used by permission. Holman Christian Standard Bible˚, Holman CSB˚, and HCSB˚ are federally registered trademarks of Holman Bible Publishers. Used by permission. All rights reserved.

Scripture quotations noted MSG are from THE MESSAGE by Eugene H. Peterson. Copyright © 1993, 1994, 1995, 1996, 2000, 2001, 2002. Used by permission of NavPress

CONTENTS

WELCOME TO
DARING FAITH: THE KEY TO MIRACLES

Jesus said, *"According to your faith will it be done to you"* (Matthew 9:29 NIV). That's an amazing statement. Jesus is saying that you get to choose how much God blesses your life. You get to choose how much God uses you in his plan for the world. How? "According to your faith will it be done to you." Faith is the key to fulfilling God's will in your life.

As we celebrate our 35th year at Saddleback Church, I am so excited about the opportunities that are ahead of us to change the world for the glory of God. They are absolutely mind boggling, but they will require daring faith.

When I think back about where we have come from, starting with just seven people in a living room, I am so humbled and amazed. We had no money, no land, no buildings, no members . . . but we did have faith that was willing to risk everything for the glory of God. And now, 35 years later, when I look at the thousands of lives that have been changed, I am overwhelmed with gratitude to God and to the people in our congregation who have prayed and served and given so faithfully and sacrificially. We have now baptized over 41,000 people at Saddleback Church. We have campuses all over Southern California and across the globe. We have over 8,000 small groups. And over 20,000 of our members have taken PEACE trips to every nation in the world. There is so much for us to celebrate! And we're just getting started.

For 35 years, Saddleback Church has been all about riding waves. We don't create the waves. God does that. We just recognize the waves, catch them, and ride them. And now as I look out on the horizon, I can see that we're about to catch the biggest wave in our history. But for us to fulfill our destiny as a church, it will require huge, courageous steps of faith. Daring faith! It will require us to prioritize and to sacrifice. It will require us to get out of our comfort zones and to move against our fears.

What about you? What wave is on your horizon? What does God want to do next in your life and your church, and how can you get ready to catch the next wave God is sending your way?

The most daring thing you can do in life is to live completely for Jesus Christ. Today in America and most of the West, we've removed all the danger of following Christ. We've made it safe, predictable, harmless and innocuous. We've made it bland and boring! Most Christians are afraid to live by their faith. They're afraid to pray brave prayers, to share a brave witness, and to take a brave stand for Jesus Christ in their ethics, their relationships, and their business practices. But where there is no risk, there is no reward! Where there is no faith, there are no miracles. Daring faith is the key to miracles in your life.

Daring faith is when you live on the edge of faith, not in the shallows of safe conformity. That's when life becomes an adventure. Your finest hours in life are when you boldly step up, step out, and take risks in Jesus' name. That's when the hero in your heart shows up and everybody notices.

God wants us to be people with daring faith—faith that refuses to hide and cower while the world goes to hell. He wants us to bravely follow our King, Jesus Christ, into the future he has planned for us.

For the next six weeks, we're going to talk about how to have daring faith both in our personal lives and in our life together as a church. The Bible says that without faith, it is impossible to please God. And what I want more than anything else for my life, for your life, and for your church is that we would all live faith-filled lives that are pleasing to God. So for the next 40 days, your faith is going to be challenged, deepened, stretched and strengthened like never before.

The next wave is coming. Let's catch it together!

Rick

HOW TO USE
THIS STUDY GUIDE

Here is a brief explanation of the features of this study guide.

- **Checking In:** Open each meeting by briefly discussing a question or two that will help focus everyone's attention on the subject of the lesson.

- **Memory Verse:** Each week you will find a key Bible verse for your group to memorize together. If someone in the group has a different translation, ask them to read it aloud so the group can get a bigger picture of the meaning of the passage.

- **Video Lesson:** There is a video lesson for the group to watch together each week. Fill in the blanks in the lesson outlines as you watch the video and be sure to refer back to these outlines during your discussion time.

- **Discovery Questions:** Each video segment is complemented by several questions for group discussion. Please don't feel pressured to discuss every single question. There is no reason to rush through the answers. Give everyone ample opportunity to share their thoughts. If you don't get through all of the discovery questions, that's okay.

- **Living on Purpose:** This is where the rubber meets the road. We don't want to be just hearers of the Word. We also need to be doers of the Word (James 1:22). In his book, *The Purpose Driven Life*, Rick Warren identifies God's five purposes for our lives. They are worship, fellowship, discipleship, ministry, and evangelism. We will focus on one or two of these five purposes in each session. These assignments are application exercises that will help you put into practice the truths you have discussed in the lesson.

- **Prayer Direction:** At the end of each session you will find suggestions for your group prayer time. Praying together is one of the greatest privileges of small group life. Please don't take it for granted.

- **Diving Deeper:** This section includes assignments for the group to complete between meetings.

- **Daily Devotions and Journal Pages:** There are seven daily devotions and seven journal pages at the end of each session in your study guide. Use these for your daily quiet times throughout the week.

- **Small Group Resources:** There are additional small group resources, such as Group Guidelines, Helps for Hosts, Prayer and Praise Reports, etc., in the back of this study guide.

- *Daring Faith* **Instagram Challenge:** At the end of each session there's an idea for an Instagram post. Keep the conversation going!

- **Before You Go:** This section includes suggestions to keep your small group organized and moving forward.

A TIP FOR THE HOST

The study guide material is meant to be your servant, not your master. The point is not to race through the sessions; the point is to take time to let God work in your lives. It is not necessary to "go around the circle" before you move on to the next question. Give people the freedom to speak, but don't insist on it. Your group will enjoy deeper, more open sharing and discussion if people don't feel pressured to speak up.

BUILDING A LIFE OF FAITH

◉ CHECKING IN

- If this is your group's first meeting, or if you have any new group members, be sure to introduce yourselves. Review the *Small Group Guidelines* on page 148 of this study guide.

- Share with the group what you are hoping to get out of this *Daring Faith* study.

◉ MEMORY VERSE

"According to your faith will it be done to you." MATTHEW 9:29 (NIV)

◉ WATCH THE VIDEO LESSON NOW AND FOLLOW ALONG IN YOUR OUTLINE.

⊛ BUILDING A LIFE OF FAITH

"According to your faith will it be done to you." MATTHEW 9:29 (NIV)

You get to choose how much God blesses your life and uses you in his plan for the world. Daring faith is the key to fulfilling God's will.

Where there is no faith, there are no miracles. Daring faith is the key to miracles in your life.

- **Faith is _____ when I don't see it.**

   "Faith is being sure of what we hope for and certain of what we do not see." HEBREWS 11:1 (NIV)

- **Faith is _____ when I don't understand it.**

   "It was by faith that Noah built an ark to save his family from the flood. He obeyed God who warned him about something that had never happened before." HEBREWS 11:7 (NLT)

   "It was faith that made Abraham obey when God called him to go out to a country which God had promised to give him. He left his own country without knowing where he was going." HEBREWS 11:8 (TEV)

- **Faith is _____ when I don't have it.**

   "It was faith that made Abel offer to God a better sacrifice than Cain's. Through his faith he won God's approval . . ." HEBREWS 11:4 (TEV)

- **Faith is _____ when I don't feel like it.**

"It was by faith that [Moses] left Egypt without fear of the king's anger; he held to his purpose like someone who could see the invisible." HEBREWS 11:27 (NJB)

- **Faith is _____ before I receive it.**

"By faith the walls of Jericho fell, after the people had marched around them for seven days." HEBREWS 11:30 (NIV)

If you wait until after a prayer has been answered to thank God, that's gratitude, but it's not faith. Faith is thanking God that the answer is already on its way, even before you see it.

- **Faith is _____ if I don't get it.**

God is more interested in your character than your comfort. He is more interested in making you holy than making you happy. So sometimes he gives you the ability to handle trials instead of removing them from your life.

"The world was not worthy of them . . . These were all commended for their faith, yet none of them received what had been promised. God had planned something better." HEBREWS 11:38-40 (NIV)

"Faith comes by hearing, and hearing by the word of God." ROMANS 10:17 (NKJV)

"These trials are only to test your faith . . . So if your faith remains strong after being tried in the test tube of fiery trials, it will bring you much praise and glory and honor on the day of his return."
1 PETER 1:7 (TLB)

DISCOVERY QUESTIONS

- Please don't feel pressured to discuss every discovery question. It's okay to choose the questions that are right for your group. The point is not to race through the session; the point is to take time to let God work in your lives.

- On a scale of 1-10, with 1 being "nonexistent" and 10 being "absolutely unshakeable," how would you rate the strength of your faith today?

- Of the six facets of faith Pastor Rick described, which one do you want to strengthen first and why? What practical step can you take this week to move in that direction?

- Who do you know that demonstrates strong faith? What lesson can you learn from their example?

- How have you seen God do something extraordinary, even miraculous, in your life or in the life of someone you know? How has that experience impacted the way you think about faith?

LIVING ON PURPOSE

This is where the rubber meets the road. We don't want to be just hearers of the Word. We also need to be doers of the Word (James 1:22). In his book, *The Purpose Driven Life*, Rick Warren identifies God's five purposes for our lives. They are worship, fellowship, discipleship, ministry, and evangelism. We will focus on one or two of these five purposes in each session. These assignments are application exercises that will help you put into practice the truths you have discussed in the lesson.

- **Worship:** Faith is thanking God that the answer is already on its way, even before you see it. What do you need to begin thanking God for today?

- **Fellowship:** Who do you know who needs to have their faith built up? Why not invite them to join your group? It's not too late.

PRAYER DIRECTION

If there are more than eight people in your group, we recommend that you break into sub-groups of three or four people by gender. This will give everyone ample time to share and pray together. If praying in a group is new or uncomfortable for you, we encourage you to start by praying single sentence prayers. Don't worry about how fancy you sound. God isn't looking for eloquence. He just wants honesty. Talk to God like you talk to a friend. Give everyone a chance to pray, but don't insist on it. Over time, you will all feel much more comfortable praying together.

Pray for each other's prayer requests. Be sure to record them on the *Small Group Prayer and Praise Report* on page 151 of this study guide. Commit to pray for each other's requests every day this week.

- Discuss how your group would like to communicate urgent prayer requests that may come up between meetings.

DIVING DEEPER

- Read the *Daring Faith* daily devotions for days 1-7 in this study guide. Write your thoughts and prayers on the journal pages. If it's more convenient, you can also listen to the daily devotions at **www.drivetimedevotions.com**. They're free!

- Read the Memory Verse on page 11 every day this week as part of your quiet time. See if you can memorize it before your next group meeting.

DARING FAITH INSTAGRAM CHALLENGE

- We dare you to share a picture of your small group. **#DaringFaith**

BEFORE YOU GO

- Turn to the *Small Group Calendar* on page 152 of this study guide. Healthy groups share responsibilities and group ownership. Fill out the calendar together, noting where you will meet each week, who will facilitate your meeting, and who will provide a meal or snack. Note special events, socials, or days off as well. Your Small Group Host will be very appreciative and everyone will have a lot more fun together. This would be a great role for someone to coordinate for the group.

- Collect basic contact information such as phone numbers and email addresses for your group members. The *Small Group Roster* on page 155 of your study guide is a good place to record this information.

NOTES

DAILY DEVOTIONS: DAY ONE
LET GOD EMPOWER YOUR PURPOSE

"I have learned the secret of living in every situation, whether it is with a full stomach or empty, with plenty or little. For I can do everything through Christ, who gives me strength."

PHILIPPIANS 4:12-13 (NLT)

You need more than positive thinking to live a life of faith. You need the power of God. The Apostle Paul says it like this: *"I have learned the secret of living in every situation, whether it is with a full stomach or empty, with plenty or little. For I can do everything through Christ, who gives me strength"* (Philippians 4:12-13 NLT).

In other words, you can do anything—with God's help.

A man came to Jesus and asked him to heal his son. He said, *"If you can do anything, take pity on us and help us."* Jesus said, *"'If you can'? Everything is possible for him who believes."* Immediately the boy's father exclaimed, *"I do believe; help me overcome my unbelief!"* (Mark 9:22-24 NIV). That's one of my favorite prayers in the Bible. It's so honest! And that's what God wants from you in prayer—honesty. If you pray that prayer, *"I do believe; help me overcome my unbelief,"* God will answer. He wants you to be strong in your faith. He wants you to overcome your unbelief.

Faith means we believe that Jesus can do what we ask, and that with his help, we can do what he asks us to do too.

Have you been trying to live life on your own power? If so, I guarantee you're getting nowhere—at least on the things that really matter in life. You can read all the motivational books in the world and still never make any progress toward your dreams. You need the supernatural help of God to live a life of faith. Surrendering your life to Jesus is the safest decision you'll ever make. It will teach you to trust God, and it will stretch your faith as you see that indeed you *"can do everything through Christ,"* who gives you strength.

WHAT DID YOU HEAR?

What did God say to you as you read today's Scripture and devotion?

_____

_____

_____

WHAT DO YOU THINK?

How does it apply to your life?

_____

_____

_____

WHAT WILL YOU DO?

Don't just be a hearer of the word. Be a doer of the word. (James 1:22)

_____

_____

_____

NOW TALK TO GOD

This is where you turn your thoughts into prayer. It could be a prayer of gratitude or praise. It could be a prayer of confession or a request for God's help. It's up to you. Take a minute to write a prayer of response to what God said to you.

_____

_____

_____

_____

DAILY DEVOTIONS: DAY TWO
FAITH COMES FROM HEARING GOD'S WORD

"Faith comes by hearing, and hearing by the Word of God."
ROMANS 10:17 (NKJV)

A gardener can plant the same kind of seed in three different locations and get three different results. In one spot, she'll get giant tomatoes. In another, she'll get small tomatoes. And in a third, she'll get nothing. What's the difference? It's not the seed, it's the soil. The soil must be prepared for the seed.

The same is true when you hear God's Word. It's why you can take two people to church, sit them side-by-side, and one will walk out thinking God really spoke to him, while the other won't get anything out of the service. The heart of one person was prepared; the other's heart wasn't.

How can you prepare the soil of your heart for the Word? The Bible says, *"Everyone should be quick to listen, slow to speak and slow to become angry, because human anger does not produce the righteousness that God desires. Therefore, get rid of all moral filth and the evil that is so prevalent and humbly accept the word planted in you, which can save you"* (James 1:19b-21 NIV).

For good reception, this passage teaches you to have four attitudes:

- **You must be quiet.** *"Be quick to listen, slow to speak."* You can't hear God if you're doing all the talking.

- **You must be calm.** *"Slow to become angry."* If you're frantic, you're not going to hear God. The Bible says, *"Be still and know that I am God"* (Psalm 46:10 NIV). My translation of that is: "Sit down and shut up."

- **You must be clean.** *"Get rid of all moral filth and evil."* Before you can meet with God, you need to take out some emotional and spiritual garbage. Get rid of the stuff that stinks in your life. You get rid of the garbage by confessing your sin to God and agreeing with him that what you did was wrong.

- **You must be humble.** *"Humbly accept the word planted in you."* Be ready to do whatever God tells you from his Word. A prideful attitude makes a hard heart.

How's your soil today?

WHAT DID YOU HEAR?

What did God say to you as you read today's Scripture and devotion?

_____

_____

_____

WHAT DO YOU THINK?

How does it apply to your life?

_____

_____

_____

WHAT WILL YOU DO?

Don't just be a hearer of the word. Be a doer of the word. (James 1:22)

_____

_____

_____

NOW TALK TO GOD

This is where you turn your thoughts into prayer. It could be a prayer of gratitude or praise. It could be a prayer of confession or a request for God's help. It's up to you. Take a minute to write a prayer of response to what God said to you.

_____

_____

_____

_____

DAILY DEVOTIONS: DAY THREE
FAITH MEANS I TRUST IN GOD'S PROMISES

"All these people earned a good reputation because of their faith, yet none of them received all that God had promised. For God had something better in mind for us, so that they would not reach perfection without us."
HEBREWS 11:39-40 (NLT)

It's not easy to live by faith. We live in a broken world. When God kicked Adam out of Eden, he told Adam that life would be hard. And it is. There's a cosmic battle for your life going on both inside and outside of you. The weather doesn't work right. Our bodies don't work right. Our relationships don't work right. You battle with your own sinful nature. You also battle against Satan himself, who wants nothing more than to "steal, kill, and destroy." And sometimes it just gets to us. We just want to give up.

But in Hebrews 11, God urges us to hang on. God hasn't forgotten us, and he will fulfill his promises one day. He promises to give us a future and a hope (Jeremiah 29:11). He promises to take away our tears (Revelation 7:17). And he gives us many other promises throughout his Word.

Hebrews 11 mentions a variety of biblical heroes who demonstrated faith in God's promises: Abraham, Isaac, Jacob, Moses, Gideon, Samson, and David, just to name a few. Though they endured many difficulties, they kept going in their spiritual journeys.

Then Hebrews 11:39-40 says, *"All these people earned a good reputation because of their faith, yet none of them received all that God had promised. For God had something better in mind for us, so that they would not reach perfection without us."*

When you feel like giving up, remember the heroes of the Bible and imitate their faith. One day, your faith and theirs will be rewarded, and we will all reach perfection together.

WHAT DID YOU HEAR?

What did God say to you as you read today's Scripture and devotion?

_____

_____

_____

WHAT DO YOU THINK?

How does it apply to your life?

_____

_____

_____

WHAT WILL YOU DO?

Don't just be a hearer of the word. Be a doer of the word. (James 1:22)

_____

_____

_____

NOW TALK TO GOD

This is where you turn your thoughts into prayer. It could be a prayer of gratitude or praise. It could be a prayer of confession or a request for God's help. It's up to you. Take a minute to write a prayer of response to what God said to you.

_____

_____

_____

_____

DAILY DEVOTIONS: DAY FOUR
FAITH MEANS I REFUSE TO GIVE UP

"Therefore, since we are surrounded by such a huge crowd of witnesses to the life of faith . . ."
HEBREWS 12:1 (NLT)

What do you do when you feel like giving up? We all have those moments when we just can't see any light at the end of the tunnel. We've been struggling with something—maybe a health issue, a broken relationship, financial problems, or depression—and we start to wonder if we have the strength to keep going.

If you find yourself at that point today, I want to share some encouragement with you from Hebrews 12 and give you a powerful reason to keep on keeping on.

Hebrews 11 is the "faith chapter" that tells us about great people of the faith: Abraham, Moses, David, and many others. Their stories are sources of encouragement in and of themselves. But a phrase that starts off the first verse of the next chapter is what I want to focus on. Hebrews 12:1 says, *"Therefore, since we are surrounded by such a huge crowd of witnesses to the life of faith . . ."*

God is saying, "Don't give up, because heaven is watching and cheering for you." That's encouraging news!

You have an audience. Nothing you do is private. Nothing you have ever done has been hidden from heaven. God sees it all. As Job says, *"He sees everything I do and every step I take"* (Job 31:4 TLB). And Jesus tells us, *"Every hair on your head has been counted"* (Luke 12:7 GW). God knows every detail of your life. He watches every breath you take. There is nothing about you that he doesn't already know. And he loves you in spite of it all!

And it's not just God who's watching. Abraham, Jacob, Moses and all the other saints are there as well. How is this encouraging? When you start to get discouraged, remember that people who have gone through much worse circumstances are watching to see how well you're enduring. And they're cheering you on from the grandstands of heaven!

WHAT DID YOU HEAR?

What did God say to you as you read today's Scripture and devotion?

_____

_____

_____

WHAT DO YOU THINK?

How does it apply to your life?

_____

_____

_____

WHAT WILL YOU DO?

Don't just be a hearer of the word. Be a doer of the word. (James 1:22)

_____

_____

_____

NOW TALK TO GOD

This is where you turn your thoughts into prayer. It could be a prayer of gratitude or praise. It could be a prayer of confession or a request for God's help. It's up to you. Take a minute to write a prayer of response to what God said to you.

_____

_____

_____

_____

DAILY DEVOTIONS: DAY FIVE
GRATITUDE BUILDS MY FAITH

"Sink your roots in him and build on him. Be strengthened by the faith that you were taught, and overflow with thanksgiving."
COLOSSIANS 2:7 (GW)

Anybody can thank God in good times. But if you can thank God even in the bad times—when life doesn't make sense and your prayers go unanswered— your faith will grow stronger and your roots will go deeper. Gratitude helps you remember the faith-lessons that God has already taught you. It helps you *"sink your roots in him and build on him,"* and to *"be strengthened by the faith that you were taught."*

When the Old Testament prophet Habakkuk went through tough times, he said, *"Though the fig tree does not bud and there are no grapes on the vines, though the olive crop fails and the fields produce no food, though there are no sheep in the pen and no cattle in the stalls, yet I will rejoice in the LORD, I will be joyful in God my Savior"* (Habakkuk 3:17-18 NIV).

In the midst of his trouble, Habakkuk rejoiced. What was the cause of his gratitude? *"I will be joyful in God my Savior."* When everything else stinks in life, you can be grateful because the Lord is your Savior. You can be thankful to God just for being God. He has promised to see you through those tough situations, and your faith will grow even stronger because of it. Just say, "God, I know you're in control. I know you love me, and I know you can bring good out of this. I'm thankful that you're bigger than my problem."

That is the ultimate test of the depth of your faith. Can you thank God when life stinks? When you're going through tough times, don't look at what's lost. Look at what's left, and be grateful for it!

WHAT DID YOU HEAR?

What did God say to you as you read today's Scripture and devotion?

_____

_____

_____

WHAT DO YOU THINK?

How does it apply to your life?

_____

_____

_____

WHAT WILL YOU DO?

Don't just be a hearer of the word. Be a doer of the word. (James 1:22)

_____

_____

_____

NOW TALK TO GOD

This is where you turn your thoughts into prayer. It could be a prayer of gratitude or praise. It could be a prayer of confession or a request for God's help. It's up to you. Take a minute to write a prayer of response to what God said to you.

_____

_____

_____

_____

DAILY DEVOTIONS: DAY SIX
GIVING TO GOD STRENGTHENS MY FAITH

"Bring all the tithes into the storehouse . . .
If you do," says the Lord of Heaven's Armies, "I will open
the windows of heaven for you. I will pour out a blessing
so great you won't have enough room to take it in!
Try it! Put me to the test!"
MALACHI 3:10 (NLT)

God uses finances to test your faith. Have you ever had to decide between paying a bill and tithing? You only have so much money—where is it going to go? This is a test. God is saying, "Do you really believe that I can take care of your bills? Or do you think you have to take care of them on your own?"

He says, *"Bring all the tithes into the storehouse . . . If you do, I will open the windows of heaven for you. I will pour out a blessing so great you won't have enough room to take it in! Try it! Put me to the test!"* In essence, God is saying, "I dare you! I dare you to see what I will do if you become a giving, generous person. Tithe, and see what happens to your life."

Did you know there are more promises in the Bible about giving than any other subject? Jesus talked more about giving than he did about heaven and hell combined. I believe this is because giving is the essence of being like Jesus. In fact, the Bible says God is a giver: *"God so loved the world that he gave . . ."* (John 3:16 NIV).

When we give, it shows God that we trust him and believe his promises to provide for us. Giving strengthens, stretches, and tests our faith.

Do you really believe God will take care of your bills? If you're struggling in this area, ask God to help you in your unbelief. Then take a step of daring faith and begin tithing. He wants to help you find the freedom in your finances that only comes from trusting in him. As you pray about your financial needs, write them down and then watch to see how God provides.

WHAT DID YOU HEAR?

What did God say to you as you read today's Scripture and devotion?

_____

_____

_____

WHAT DO YOU THINK?

How does it apply to your life?

_____

_____

_____

WHAT WILL YOU DO?

Don't just be a hearer of the word. Be a doer of the word. (James 1:22)

_____

_____

_____

NOW TALK TO GOD

This is where you turn your thoughts into prayer. It could be a prayer of gratitude or praise. It could be a prayer of confession or a request for God's help. It's up to you. Take a minute to write a prayer of response to what God said to you.

_____

_____

_____

_____

DAILY DEVOTIONS: DAY SEVEN
FAITH = LOVE + TRUST + ACTION

"If you love me, you will obey what I command."
JOHN 14:15 (NIV)

The word "obey" has a negative connotation today. We view obedience as a forced, unwilling decision to do something we don't want to do because we're afraid of punishment. But that's not the kind of obedience God wants from us.

Obedience is not about being afraid of God, but about being in a loving relationship with God. As Jesus said in John 14:15: *"If you love me, you will obey what I command."* Obedience comes from knowing that God loves you and loving him in return.

Out of love comes trust. If you know God loves you and you love him, then you will trust what God is saying to you.

Then trust will lead to action. This is the essence of living by faith: We believe God loves us and we love him back, we trust what he tells us, and that leads us to live the way God wants us to live.

Love without action is just mere talk, and action without love is just rote religion.

Think about the story of Joseph, the earthly father of Jesus. He wasn't convinced that Mary was telling the truth about how she became pregnant, but an angel told Joseph to believe her. The baby would be the Savior of his people.

Joseph accepted the truth because of his relationship with God. He knew God loved him, and he loved God. He trusted God and made the choice to do what God asked him to do, even though he didn't understand what was happening. And that choice changed everything.

Think about this: In an instant, Joseph's whole world was turned upside down. Because he loved God, trusted God, and obeyed God, Joseph stepped into the destiny that God had planned for him.

Faith = Love + Trust + Action. Do you love God? Do you trust him? Then take action and do what he tells you to do.

WHAT DID YOU HEAR?

What did God say to you as you read today's Scripture and devotion?

_____

_____

_____

WHAT DO YOU THINK?

How does it apply to your life?

_____

_____

_____

WHAT WILL YOU DO?

Don't just be a hearer of the word. Be a doer of the word. (James 1:22)

_____

_____

_____

NOW TALK TO GOD

This is where you turn your thoughts into prayer. It could be a prayer of gratitude or praise. It could be a prayer of confession or a request for God's help. It's up to you. Take a minute to write a prayer of response to what God said to you.

_____

_____

_____

_____

EXPECTING THE BEST

CHECKING IN

- In our last session, you rated the strength of your faith on a scale of 1-10. Did anything happen this week that increased your faith to a higher number?

- Share a verse or insight that was especially meaningful to you in your Daring Faith daily devotions this past week.

MEMORY VERSE

"And we know that in all things God works for the good of those who love him, who have been called according to his purpose." ROMANS 8:28 (NIV)

WATCH THE VIDEO LESSON NOW AND FOLLOW ALONG IN YOUR OUTLINE.

⊛ EXPECTING THE BEST

"Faith assures us of things we expect and convinces us of the existence of things we cannot see." **HEBREWS 11:1 (GW)**

Faith is not just optimism or positive thinking. Faith is the confident assurance that God is in control of the future, and that he plans what is best for my life because he loves me.

"I will guide you along the best pathway for your life. I will advise you and watch over you." **PSALM 32:8 (NLT)**

- **When I expect the best it _____ God.**

    "This day the Lord will hand you over to me and I'll strike you down and the whole world will know that there is a God!" **1 SAMUEL 17:46 (NIV)**

    "Expect great things from God, and attempt great things for God."
    —William Carey

- **When I expect the best it _____ my ability.**

- **When I expect the best it _____ others.**

If I want to expect the best from God, I must:

- **_____ every morning.**

    "In the morning, O Lord, you hear my voice; in the morning I lay my requests before you and wait in expectation." **PSALM 5:3 (NIV)**

- _____ **throughout the day.**

"Though the wicked hide along the way to kill me, I will quietly keep my mind upon your promises." PSALM 119:95 (TLB)

"I've banked your promises in the vault of my heart." PSALM 119:11 (MSG)

"Let's keep a firm grip on the promises that keep us going. [God] always keeps his word." HEBREWS 10:23 (TLB)

- _____ **even when things look bad.**

"O my soul, don't be discouraged. Don't be upset. Expect God to act! For I know that I shall again have plenty of reason to praise him for all that he will do." PSALM 42:11 (TLB)

- _____ **other believers.**

"Bad company corrupts good character." 1 CORINTHIANS 15:33 (NLT)

"Let us not give up the habit of meeting together . . . Instead, let us encourage one another all the more." HEBREWS 10:25 (TEV)

"Let us consider how we may spur one another on toward love and good deeds." HEBREWS 10:24 (NIV)

"Without faith it is impossible to please God." HEBREWS 11:6 (NIV)

DISCOVERY QUESTIONS

- What Goliath are you up against right now? How has learning about the power of expecting the best in faith encouraged you to approach that giant in a different way?

- David developed a daily spiritual routine by tuning in to God, thinking on his promises, trusting God's love, and talking with other believers. Which of these four disciplines is easiest for you? Which one is more difficult and why? What practical step will you take this week to begin strengthening yourself in that area of spiritual discipline?

- When you expect the best in faith, it honors God, increases your ability, and encourages others. Share an experience when you expected the best from God and how your attitude encouraged another person.

- What is the difference between biblical faith and positive thinking?

LIVING ON PURPOSE

- **Ministry:** Who do you know that is facing a Goliath right now? How can you encourage them this week with the truths you learned in this session? Send them a text or email right now and tell them you are praying for them. Then make a note in your calendar to give them a call, pay them a visit, or send them a note of encouragement this week.

  Who has been a VIP—Very Inspirational Person—in your life? How have they encouraged you in your faith? Send them a thank you note, text, or email this week.

PRAYER DIRECTION

- Faith is the confident assurance that God is in control, and that he plans what is best for your life because he loves you. Before you pray for your requests, spend a few minutes thanking God for his power—"God is in control," his wisdom—"he plans what is best for your life," and his love—"because he loves you."

- Pray for each other's prayer requests. Be sure to record them on the *Small Group Prayer and Praise Report* on page 151 of this study guide. Commit to pray for each other's requests every day this week.

DIVING DEEPER

- Read the *Daring Faith* daily devotions for days 8-14 in this study guide. Write your thoughts and prayers on the journal pages. If it's more convenient, you can also listen to the daily devotions at **www.drivetimedevotions.com**. They're free!

- Read the Memory Verse on page 33 every day this week as part of your quiet time. See if you can memorize it before your next group meeting.

DARING FAITH INSTAGRAM CHALLENGE

- We dare you to share a picture of your quiet time spot. **#DaringFaith**

NOTES

_____

_____

_____

_____

_____

_____

_____

_____

_____

_____

_____

_____

_____

_____

_____

_____

_____

_____

_____

_____

_____

NOTES

_____

_____

_____

_____

_____

_____

_____

_____

_____

_____

_____

_____

_____

_____

_____

_____

_____

_____

_____

_____

_____

_____

DAILY DEVOTIONS: DAY EIGHT
EXPECT THE BEST: GOD IS AT WORK

"And we know that in all things God works for the good of those who love him, who have been called according to his purpose."
ROMANS 8:28 (NIV)

Do you ever find yourself asking, "Why is life so hard?" Frustration is the result of living in a world that is broken by sin. You can't avoid suffering. There will be pain. There will be days of doubt. And that's exactly the time you should expect the best from God, and declare in faith *"that in all things God works for the good of those who love him, who have been called according to his purpose"* (Romans 8:28 NIV).

No matter how bad the situation may seem, the Bible says you can be sure God is still in control and that God is working things out for your good. If you want to expect the best from God, remember these four truths:

- **The Holy Spirit is praying for you.** *"The Spirit himself speaks to God for us, even begs God for us with deep feelings that words cannot explain"* (Romans 8:26 NCV).

- **God uses everything for your good.** *"And we know that in all things God works for the good of those who love him"* (Romans 8:28 NIV). God is bigger than your enemies. He's bigger than your critics. He's bigger than your problems. And he's working it all for good in your life.

- **God wants you to succeed.** *"If God is for us, who can ever be against us?"* (Romans 8:31 NLT). God wants you to succeed in all those areas where you are failing. He's pulling for you.

- **God will give you what you need.** *"Since God did not spare even his own Son but gave him up for us all, won't God, who gave us Christ, also give us everything else?"* (Romans 8:32 NLT). God solved your biggest problem when he paid for all your sins, including the sins you haven't done yet. If God cared enough to save you and give you the gift of eternal life, don't you think he cares about the problems in your daily life? If it's big enough to worry about, it's big enough to pray about. And if you pray about it, you won't have to worry about it.

WHAT DID YOU HEAR?

What did God say to you as you read today's Scripture and devotion?

_____

_____

_____

WHAT DO YOU THINK?

How does it apply to your life?

_____

_____

_____

WHAT WILL YOU DO?

Don't just be a hearer of the word. Be a doer of the word. (James 1:22)

_____

_____

_____

NOW TALK TO GOD

This is where you turn your thoughts into prayer. It could be a prayer of gratitude or praise. It could be a prayer of confession or a request for God's help. It's up to you. Take a minute to write a prayer of response to what God said to you.

_____

_____

_____

_____

DAILY DEVOTIONS: DAY NINE
EXPECT GOD TO ANSWER YOUR PRAYERS

"If you want to know what God wants you to do,
ask him, for he is always ready to give a bountiful
supply of wisdom to all who ask him . . . But when you ask
him, be sure that you really expect him to tell you . . .
If you don't ask with faith, don't expect the Lord to give
you any solid answer."
JAMES 1:5-8 (TLB)

God wants to direct you in life, but two things need to line up: You have to ask the right person—God, and you have to ask with the right attitude—in faith, expecting an answer.

Have you ever asked God for something but didn't expect to get it? That's why you didn't get it. God works in our lives according to faith. So many times we say, "God, please guide me!" and we walk away not even waiting for guidance. We just immediately start to work. We say, "God, I want you to give me wisdom; help me make the right decision." But we don't really expect him to do that. We think it all depends on us. But the Bible says, *"When you ask him, be sure that you really expect him to tell you"* (James 1:6 TLB).

Wisdom is seeing life from God's point of view. Wisdom is the ability to make decisions the way God makes decisions. God has promised to give you wisdom, if you will ask. *"If you want to know what God wants you to do, ask him, for he is always ready to give a bountiful supply of wisdom to all who ask him"* (James 1:5 TLB).

Think about this: God never makes a bad decision. He never makes a mistake. He says if you trust him and listen to him, he will guide you. But you must ask in faith. *"If you don't ask with faith, don't expect the Lord to give you any solid answer"* (James 1:8 TLB).

Where do you need wisdom today? Ask God what you should do, and then expect him to tell you. Give him time to answer your prayer.

WHAT DID YOU HEAR?

What did God say to you as you read today's Scripture and devotion?

_____

_____

_____

WHAT DO YOU THINK?

How does it apply to your life?

_____

_____

_____

WHAT WILL YOU DO?

Don't just be a hearer of the word. Be a doer of the word. (James 1:22)

_____

_____

_____

NOW TALK TO GOD

This is where you turn your thoughts into prayer. It could be a prayer of gratitude or praise. It could be a prayer of confession or a request for God's help. It's up to you. Take a minute to write a prayer of response to what God said to you.

_____

_____

_____

_____

DAILY DEVOTIONS: DAY TEN
WAITING FOR ANSWERED PRAYER

"Because the Sovereign Lord helps me, I will not be disgraced. Therefore, I have set my face like a stone, determined to do his will. And I know that I will not be put to shame."
ISAIAH 50:7 (NLT)

When you pray, expect to hear from God. I can't say it any simpler than that. Expect that God will answer your prayer. This is where faith comes in. You wait expectantly on God, *"set like a stone, determined to do his will"* (Isaiah 50:7).

Waiting on God is never a waste of time. In fact, it is time well invested in your life. It keeps you focused on God and living in light of eternity.

Hurry is the death of prayer. One reason you may not hear God speak to you is that you don't wait long enough. He wants you to care enough to listen. He wants to be sure you are paying attention. And sometimes he has to wait for you to calm down so that he can get a word in edgewise.

The Bible says there are three things to do as you wait:

- **Wait quietly:** *"Let all that I am wait quietly before God, for my hope is in him"* (Psalm 62:5 NLT).

- **Wait patiently:** *"Be still in the presence of the Lord, and wait patiently for him to act"* (Psalm 37:7 NLT).

- **Wait expectantly:** *"I wait expectantly, trusting God to help, for he has promised"* (Psalm 130:5 TLB).

When you pray, wait quietly, patiently, and expectantly to hear from God. He promises you will not be disgraced or put to shame.

WHAT DID YOU HEAR?

What did God say to you as you read today's Scripture and devotion?

_____

_____

_____

WHAT DO YOU THINK?

How does it apply to your life?

_____

_____

_____

WHAT WILL YOU DO?

Don't just be a hearer of the word. Be a doer of the word. (James 1:22)

_____

_____

_____

NOW TALK TO GOD

This is where you turn your thoughts into prayer. It could be a prayer of gratitude or praise. It could be a prayer of confession or a request for God's help. It's up to you. Take a minute to write a prayer of response to what God said to you.

_____

_____

_____

_____

DAILY DEVOTIONS: DAY ELEVEN
TRUST GOD TO USE YOUR PROBLEMS FOR GOOD

"We were crushed and overwhelmed beyond our ability to endure, and we thought we would never live through it. In fact, we expected to die. But as a result, we stopped relying on ourselves and learned to rely only on God, who raises the dead."
2 CORINTHIANS 1:8-9 (NLT)

None of us are exempt from suffering. We all experience loneliness, criticism, discouragement, and mistreatment. Why does God allow these things to happen to us? It's because God is developing the character of Christ within us, and in order to do that, he must take us through the circumstances in life that he took Jesus through.

Did Jesus suffer? Was Jesus sometimes lonely? Was he tempted to be discouraged? Was he misunderstood, maligned, and criticized unjustly? Of course! Does this mean God causes tragedies? No. God is good. He will not cause evil or do evil. But God can use dark and stressful times for your good.

He'll use them to teach you to trust him: *"We stopped relying on ourselves and learned to rely only on God"* (2 Corinthians 1:8-9).

He'll use them to show you how to help others: *"He comforts us in all our troubles so that we can comfort others. When they are troubled, we will be able to give them the same comfort God has given us"* (2 Corinthians 1:4).

And he'll use them to draw you closer to other believers: *"You are helping us by praying for us . . . Many people will give thanks because God has graciously answered so many prayers"* (2 Corinthians 1:11).

So how can you expect the best from God when you're going through difficult times?

- **In faith,** refuse to be discouraged, knowing that God is for you.

- **In faith,** believe God is with you and working things out for your good.

- **In faith,** rely on God's protection and guidance.

WHAT DID YOU HEAR?

What did God say to you as you read today's Scripture and devotion?

_____

_____

_____

WHAT DO YOU THINK?

How does it apply to your life?

_____

_____

_____

WHAT WILL YOU DO?

Don't just be a hearer of the word. Be a doer of the word. (James 1:22)

_____

_____

_____

NOW TALK TO GOD

This is where you turn your thoughts into prayer. It could be a prayer of gratitude or praise. It could be a prayer of confession or a request for God's help. It's up to you. Take a minute to write a prayer of response to what God said to you.

_____

_____

_____

_____

DAILY DEVOTIONS: DAY TWELVE
EXPECT GOD TO HELP YOU GROW SPIRITUALLY

"Let us not become weary in doing good, for at the proper time we will reap a harvest if we do not give up."
GALATIANS 6:9 (NIV)

When you think about your walk with Jesus, some days you may wonder, "Why is it taking so long to see progress? I'm still struggling with so many problems. When will I finally get it right?"

Spiritual growth is like the growth we see in nature—the best fruit ripens slowly. The problem is we tend to get impatient, so we dig up the seed to check the progress of its growth, and that slows down the process! If you're not seeing as much fruit as you'd like, don't despair. Growth takes time. The Bible says, *"Let us not become weary in doing good, for at the proper time we will reap a harvest if we do not give up"* (Galatians 6:9 NIV).

Try these steps toward spiritual growth:

Nurture growth with God's Word. When you read the promises of God again and again, they build your faith and renew your certainty that fruit is coming, even though you may not see it now: *"Now faith is being sure of what we hope for and certain of what we do not see"* (Hebrews 11:1 NIV).

Cooperate with God as he prunes. Praise God for the work he's doing in your life, remembering that *"he prunes the branches that do bear fruit so they will produce even more"* (John 15:2 NLT).

Pray through the "fruit list." Pray through the list of the fruit of the Spirit from Galatians 5:22-23. The NIV (New International Version) Bible lists the fruit as *"love, joy, peace, patience, kindness, goodness, faithfulness, gentleness and self-control."* Ask God to help you grow this fruit in your life. Ask him if there is anything you are doing to hinder its growth.

WHAT DID YOU HEAR?

What did God say to you as you read today's Scripture and devotion?

_____

_____

_____

WHAT DO YOU THINK?

How does it apply to your life?

_____

_____

_____

WHAT WILL YOU DO?

Don't just be a hearer of the word. Be a doer of the word. (James 1:22)

_____

_____

_____

NOW TALK TO GOD

This is where you turn your thoughts into prayer. It could be a prayer of gratitude or praise. It could be a prayer of confession or a request for God's help. It's up to you. Take a minute to write a prayer of response to what God said to you.

_____

_____

_____

_____

DAILY DEVOTIONS: DAY THIRTEEN
TRUST GOD FOR A SECOND (OR THIRD OR FOURTH) CHANCE

"By faith we have been made acceptable to God. And now, because of our Lord Jesus Christ, we live at peace with God."

ROMANS 5:1 (CEV)

Most of us could use a second chance. Sometimes even a third or fourth chance. The Good News is that Jesus is all about second chances.

Jesus said, *"I didn't come to judge the world, but to save it"* (John 3:17 NIV). That means God doesn't stand behind you and shake his head disapprovingly when you blow it. You don't need to feel ashamed about your past failures. God isn't ashamed of you.

Too many people go through life feeling guilty, judged, and criticized by God. They have no desire to spend time with the critical god they've imagined in their heads, the one they are sure is disappointed with them.

It takes faith to get past this false image and to believe that God loves you unconditionally. The truth is, Jesus died in your place on the cross, and through faith in him you are now completely acceptable to God. The Bible says, *"By faith we have been made acceptable to God. And now, because of our Lord Jesus Christ, we live at peace with God"* (Romans 5:1 CEV).

Are you at peace with God? God wants to give you his best, no matter how many times you've failed in the past. The Bible says that, through Jesus, you have complete access to God and his power in your life. You don't have to wait until you get your life together. You get all the amazing benefits of being a child of God today!

Your life will be completely transformed if you become consistently aware of God's unconditional and never-ending love for you. Instead of letting your past failures define you, my prayer is that you will fully understand God's great love for you. I pray that his love will give you the power to get up when you fall down.

WHAT DID YOU HEAR?

What did God say to you as you read today's Scripture and devotion?

_____

_____

_____

WHAT DO YOU THINK?

How does it apply to your life?

_____

_____

_____

WHAT WILL YOU DO?

Don't just be a hearer of the word. Be a doer of the word. (James 1:22)

_____

_____

_____

NOW TALK TO GOD

This is where you turn your thoughts into prayer. It could be a prayer of gratitude or praise. It could be a prayer of confession or a request for God's help. It's up to you. Take a minute to write a prayer of response to what God said to you.

_____

_____

_____

_____

DAILY DEVOTIONS: DAY FOURTEEN
HAVE YOU CLAIMED YOUR INHERITANCE?

*"I commit you to God and to the word of his grace, which
can build you up and give you an inheritance among all
those who are sanctified."*
ACTS 20:32 (NIV)

You have an inheritance coming to you. It's promised to you in the Word of
God's grace.

Pretend your father is the richest man in the world. He dies and leaves you in
his will. You would be foolish if you never took the time to read the will. You
wouldn't know what was rightfully due to you. You wouldn't benefit from what
belongs to you as a child of the world's wealthiest man.

When you become a follower of Jesus, you're not just a believer, you're a
belonger. You become a part of God's family. Family privileges come along
with that decision. The Bible says, *"Because we are united with Christ, we
have received an inheritance from God"* (Ephesians 1:11 NLT).

But this inheritance doesn't come to you when God dies—he'll never die! It
comes to you when you're born again. The Bible says, *"Praise be to the God and
Father of our Lord Jesus Christ! In his great mercy he has given us new birth
into a living hope through the resurrection of Jesus Christ from the dead, and
into an inheritance that can never perish, spoil or fade—kept in heaven for
you"* (1 Peter 1:3-4 NIV).

What is that inheritance? Part of it is the promises in God's Word. But if you
lived your entire life and never took the time to learn the benefits that were
available to you as a child of God, that would be sad—and foolish. God wants
you to know what's available to you from him.

It requires faith to receive your inheritance. You have to believe that God loves
you and accepts you as part of his family in Christ. You have to believe he will
fulfill his promises, and that your inheritance is real, not just some empty
words to make you feel good when things seem bad. Get into the Word. Find
out what is rightfully yours. And then in faith, expect the best from God.

WHAT DID YOU HEAR?

What did God say to you as you read today's Scripture and devotion?

_____

_____

_____

WHAT DO YOU THINK?

How does it apply to your life?

_____

_____

_____

WHAT WILL YOU DO?

Don't just be a hearer of the word. Be a doer of the word. (James 1:22)

_____

_____

_____

NOW TALK TO GOD

This is where you turn your thoughts into prayer. It could be a prayer of gratitude or praise. It could be a prayer of confession or a request for God's help. It's up to you. Take a minute to write a prayer of response to what God said to you.

_____

_____

_____

_____

STRETCHING YOUR IMAGINATION

⊛ CHECKING IN

- In the Living on Purpose section last week, you thought of a person you would encourage with the lessons you are learning about faith. Does anyone have a follow-up story to share?

- Share a verse or insight that was especially meaningful to you in your *Daring Faith* daily devotions this past week.

⊛ MEMORY VERSE

"No eye has seen, no ear has heard, and no mind has imagined what God has prepared for those who love him." 1 CORINTHIANS 2:9 (NLT)

⊛ WATCH THE VIDEO LESSON NOW AND FOLLOW ALONG IN YOUR OUTLINE.

🌊 STRETCHING YOUR IMAGINATION

"With God's power working in us, God can do much, much more than anything we can ask or imagine." **EPHESIANS 3:20 (NCV)**

What are you asking? What are you imagining? Are your dreams limiting what God can do in your life? The question is not "Who do you think you are?" The right question is "Who do you think God is?" Let the size of your God determine the size of your dream.

- **You must let go of** _____.

    Doubt your doubts and believe your beliefs. Doubt is always a choice.

    "Anyone who doubts is like a wave in the sea, blown up and down by the wind . . . They should not think they will receive anything from the Lord." **JAMES 1:6-7 (NCV)**

    "Be bold and strong! Banish fear and doubt! For remember, the Lord your God is with you wherever you go." **JOSHUA 1:9 (TLB)**

Two Causes of Doubt:

- _____ **my abilities.**

    "When they measure . . . and compare themselves to themselves, they show how foolish they are." **2 CORINTHIANS 10:12 (GW)**

    If God only used perfect people, nothing would ever get done.

- _____ **my failures.**

If you focus on your past mistakes and failures, you will miss out on what God wants to do in the present and in your future.

"Forgetting the past and looking forward to what lies ahead, I press on to reach the end of the race and receive the heavenly prize for which God, through Christ Jesus, is calling us." **PHILIPPIANS 3:13-14 (NLT)**

God uses people with checkered pasts. What matters is not where you have been, but where you are headed today.

- **Look for** _____.

"I promised Moses I would give you this land, so I will give you every place you go in the land." **JOSHUA 1:3 (NCV)**

"Every one of you knows . . . [that] God has given you all the good things that he promised. Every promise he has made has been kept; not one has failed." **JOSHUA 23:14 (TEV)**

Three Promises from God:

What does God promise if you say, "Lord, I want you to use my life for your purposes?"

- **God promises** _____.

"No one will be able to stand up against you." **JOSHUA 1:5 (NIV)**

- **God promises** _____.

- **God promises** _____.

"[I] will be with you wherever you go." JOSHUA 1:9 (NIV)

"Always <u>remember</u> what is written in this book. <u>Study</u> it day and night to be sure to <u>obey</u> everything that is written there. If you do this, you will be <u>wise</u> and <u>successful</u> in everything." JOSHUA 1:8 (NCV)

God's promise of success is not based on your ability. It is based on your commitment to his Word.

- **Lean on** _____.

"No one will be able to defeat you all your life. Just as I was with Moses, so I will be with you. I will not leave you or forget you." JOSHUA 1:5 (NCV)

Who or what are you leaning on for strength?

"Trust in the Lord with all your heart and don't lean on your own understanding. In all your ways acknowledge him, and he will make your paths straight." PROVERBS 3:5-6 (NIV)

- **Launch out in** _____.

"Then Joshua issued instructions to the leaders . . . to tell the people to get ready to cross the Jordan River." JOSHUA 1:10 (TLB)

What is your Jordan River? What is the barrier in your life that you think you will never get over? What is standing between you and God's dream? Courage is not the absence of fear. Courage is moving ahead in spite of your fear.

"God can do anything, you know—far more than you could ever imagine or guess or request in your wildest dreams! He does it not by pushing us around but by working within us, his Spirit deeply and gently working within us." EPHESIANS 3:20 (MSG)

DISCOVERY QUESTIONS

- Is your dream big enough for God? Are you pursuing your dream or God's dream for your life?

- Does the idea of God having a dream for your life excite you or frighten you? Explain your answer.

- "Believe your beliefs and doubt your doubts. Doubt is the enemy of God's dream for your life." What doubts do you need to dump so God can use you?

- Courage is moving ahead in spite of your fear. God is waiting for you to take a step of faith so he can bless you with a miracle. What step of daring faith do you need to take this week to pursue God's dream?

LIVING ON PURPOSE

- **Discipleship:** Joshua 1:8 tells us that if we remember the Word, study the Word, and obey the Word, we will be wise and successful. How will you prioritize and protect your daily time in the Word this week so that you can experience the richness of God's promise? Share practical suggestions with your group.

PRAYER DIRECTION

- Are you ready to stretch your imagination? 1 Samuel 3:9 (NIV) says, *"Speak, Lord, for your servant is listening."* Ask God to show each of you the next step he wants you to take to fulfill his dream for your life.

- Pray for each other's prayer requests. Be sure to record them on the *Small Group Prayer and Praise Report* on page 151 of this study guide. Commit to pray for each other's requests every day this week.

DIVING DEEPER

- Read the *Daring Faith* daily devotions for days 15-21 in this study guide. Write your thoughts and prayers on the journal pages. If it's more convenient, you can also listen to the daily devotions at **www.drivetimedevotions.com**. They're free!

- Read the Memory Verse on page 55 every day this week as part of your quiet time. See if you can memorize it before your next group meeting.

DARING FAITH INSTAGRAM CHALLENGE

- We dare you to share a dream you've had for your life. **#DaringFaith**

NOTES

DAILY DEVOTIONS: DAY FIFTEEN
RELYING ON GOD REQUIRES FAITH

"Trust in the Lord with all your heart and lean not on your own understanding; in all your ways acknowledge him, and he will make your paths straight."
PROVERBS 3:5-6 (NIV)

When you lean on something, you trust that it will hold you up. When you lean on the Lord, you are saying, "I have faith that God is strong enough to hold me up."

God told Joshua, *"No one will be able to defeat you all your life. Just as I was with Moses so I will be with you. I will not leave you or forget you"* (Joshua 1:5 NCV). And God says that to you too. As long as Joshua leaned on God, he was undefeatable. Joshua accomplished the impossible because he was depending on the Lord.

Who or what are you leaning on for strength? Are you leaning on the approval of other people? That is a very shaky foundation. People are going to let you down. Nobody can hold you up all the time. Eventually, they're going to get tired and you're going to get dropped.

You can't even trust in yourself. Have you noticed how often you let yourself down? You make promises to yourself all the time that you don't keep. So what can you do?

"Trust in the Lord with all your heart and lean not on your own understanding; in all your ways acknowledge him, and he will make your paths straight" (Proverbs 3:5-6 NIV). Leaning on the Lord can be scary. Sometimes it's uncomfortable. It can make you worry, "Is God going to come through? Is he going to hold me up?"

That's why it requires faith to lean on the Lord. You have to believe he has your best interest at heart. You have to trust him even when you don't understand, and you have to move forward convinced that he will make your paths straight.

When you do this, you will discover that *"no eye has seen, no ear has heard, and no mind has imagined what God has prepared for those who love him"* (1 Corinthians 2:9 NLT).

WHAT DID YOU HEAR?

What did God say to you as you read today's Scripture and devotion?

_____

_____

_____

WHAT DO YOU THINK?

How does it apply to your life?

_____

_____

_____

WHAT WILL YOU DO?

Don't just be a hearer of the word. Be a doer of the word. (James 1:22)

_____

_____

_____

NOW TALK TO GOD

This is where you turn your thoughts into prayer. It could be a prayer of gratitude or praise. It could be a prayer of confession or a request for God's help. It's up to you. Take a minute to write a prayer of response to what God said to you.

_____

_____

_____

_____

DAILY DEVOTIONS: DAY SIXTEEN
LET GO OF YOUR DOUBT

"Be bold and strong! Banish fear and doubt! For remember, the Lord your God is with you wherever you go."
JOSHUA 1:9 (TLB)

Doubt will cause you to miss God's best. James 1:6 (TEV) says, *"Whoever doubts is like a wave in the sea that is driven and blown about by the wind."* When you doubt, you let your circumstances control you.

There are two things that rob your confidence and cause doubt.

- **Comparing yourself to others causes doubt.** 2 Corinthians 10:12 says that people who compare themselves to other people are foolish. You should never compare yourself to anybody else because you are unique. God made you to be you; he doesn't want you to be somebody else. Most people start off in life as originals and end up as carbon copies—and poor carbon copies at that! God says not to compare yourself for two reasons: You'll either find somebody who's doing a better job than you, and you'll get discouraged, or you'll find somebody who is doing a poorer job than you, and you will be filled with pride. Don't compare yourself. You are unique, so you are incomparable!

- **Past failures cause doubt.** You might think that because of certain things in your past, God could never use you. Have you ever read the Bible? The spiritual leaders of the Bible did not exactly have stellar records. Moses was a murderer. David was an adulterer and a murderer. Abraham gave his wife away—twice! Jacob stole the family inheritance from his brother. Paul was a religious terrorist before he met Jesus. Peter was a hard driving, hard drinking, hard living fisherman—a salty sea dog! And he probably cussed like one, too. God uses people with checkered pasts because none of us are perfect. God uses average, ordinary, dysfunctional people. If God only used perfect people, nothing would get done in this world.

Believe the Bible when it says that God has a purpose for your life, and that even before you were born he had a plan to use you for ministry. So *"be bold and strong! Banish fear and doubt! For remember, the Lord your God is with you wherever you go"* (Joshua 1:9 TLB).

WHAT DID YOU HEAR?

What did God say to you as you read today's Scripture and devotion?

_____

_____

_____

WHAT DO YOU THINK?

How does it apply to your life?

_____

_____

_____

WHAT WILL YOU DO?

Don't just be a hearer of the word. Be a doer of the word. (James 1:22)

_____

_____

_____

NOW TALK TO GOD

This is where you turn your thoughts into prayer. It could be a prayer of gratitude or praise. It could be a prayer of confession or a request for God's help. It's up to you. Take a minute to write a prayer of response to what God said to you.

_____

_____

_____

_____

DAILY DEVOTIONS: DAY SEVENTEEN
STAY FAITHFUL WHEN OTHERS DOUBT YOU

"Everyone assembled here will know that the Lord rescues his people, but not with sword and spear. This is the Lord's battle, and he will give you to us!"
1 SAMUEL 17:47 (NLT)

When God gives you a dream, don't be surprised when people try to hold you back—sometimes even the people who love you the most.

David faced four giants before he got to Goliath. They weren't physical giants, but they were giants in his mind. You're going to face these giants too.

The first giant was delay. In David's case, his dad held him back. Even after the Prophet Samuel anointed David as king, Jesse told David to get back to tending sheep! No dream is fulfilled instantly. God gives you the dream one day, but he doesn't fulfill it the next day. It may be years before you see the fulfillment of your life dream. There is always a waiting period.

The second giant was discouragement. Goliath created a climate of fear in Israel. Everybody was convinced they were going to lose the battle. But David rose up in faith and said to Goliath, *"This is the Lord's battle, and he will give you to us!"* (1 Samuel 17:47 NLT). Who are you listening to who says it can't be done?

The third giant was disapproval. David's brother questioned his motives and disapproved of him going after Goliath. When God gives you a dream that other people are afraid of and you go for it anyway, you will be misjudged, maligned, and misunderstood. You have to decide what matters more to you—the approval of other people or the approval of God.

The fourth giant was doubt. There was no greater expert on war than King Saul. He told David he was crazy for thinking he could fight a warrior like Goliath. Are you doubting yourself because some "expert" is saying you can't do it, even though God says you can?

When you face delays, discouragement, disapproval, and doubt, hold on to this promise: *"This is the Lord's battle, and he will give you to us!"* (1 Samuel 17:47 NLT).

WHAT DID YOU HEAR?

What did God say to you as you read today's Scripture and devotion?

_____

_____

_____

WHAT DO YOU THINK?

How does it apply to your life?

_____

_____

_____

WHAT WILL YOU DO?

Don't just be a hearer of the word. Be a doer of the word. (James 1:22)

_____

_____

_____

NOW TALK TO GOD

This is where you turn your thoughts into prayer. It could be a prayer of gratitude or praise. It could be a prayer of confession or a request for God's help. It's up to you. Take a minute to write a prayer of response to what God said to you.

_____

_____

_____

_____

DAILY DEVOTIONS: DAY EIGHTEEN
BECOMING A PERSON OF GREAT FAITH

"You come against me with sword and spear and javelin, but I come against you in the name of the Lord Almighty . . . This day the Lord will hand you over to me . . . and the whole world will know that there is a God in Israel."

1 SAMUEL 17:45-46 (NIV)

How do you face the fears that keep you from becoming the believer God wants you to be? If you want to be a person of great faith, do what David did.

Remember how God has helped you in the past. In 1 Samuel 17:37 (NLT), David said, *"The Lord who rescued me from the claws of the lion and the bear will rescue me from this Philistine!"* When you remember how God has helped you in the past, it gives you confidence and greater faith for the future.

Use the tools God gives you. King Saul tried to give David his own armor, but it didn't fit. Instead, David *"picked up five smooth stones from a stream and put them into his shepherd's bag. Then, armed only with his shepherd's staff and sling, he started across the valley to fight the Philistine"* (1 Samuel 17:39-40 NLT).

Don't wait for something you don't have—money, education, or connections—before you step out in faith. Use the tools God has already given you to face your giants with confidence.

Expect God to help you for his glory. David stormed the battlefield, shouting, *"You come against me with sword and spear and javelin, but I come against you in the name of the Lord Almighty . . . This day the Lord will hand you over to me . . . and the whole world will know that there is a God in Israel"* (1 Samuel 17:45-46 NIV).

What God calls you to do, he will enable and empower you to do. Follow David's example: remember how God has helped you in the past, use the tools God gives you, and expect God to help you for his glory.

WHAT DID YOU HEAR?

What did God say to you as you read today's Scripture and devotion?

_____

_____

_____

WHAT DO YOU THINK?

How does it apply to your life?

_____

_____

_____

WHAT WILL YOU DO?

Don't just be a hearer of the word. Be a doer of the word. (James 1:22)

_____

_____

_____

NOW TALK TO GOD

This is where you turn your thoughts into prayer. It could be a prayer of gratitude or praise. It could be a prayer of confession or a request for God's help. It's up to you. Take a minute to write a prayer of response to what God said to you.

_____

_____

_____

_____

DAILY DEVOTIONS: DAY NINETEEN
STEP FORWARD IN FAITH

"For our life is a matter of faith, not of sight."
2 CORINTHIANS 5:7 (TEV)

Are you waiting for God to do something? Has it occurred to you that maybe God is waiting for you to do something first? Throughout the Bible we see an important truth: The Holy Spirit releases his power the moment you take a step of faith.

When God says go, he doesn't mean stop. When he says now, he doesn't mean later. God told Joshua to cross the Jordan River when it was at flood stage. He didn't tell him to wait until the torrent had subsided. That's typical of God. He tests your faith when things look overwhelming.

When Joshua faced an impassible barrier, the floodwaters of the Jordan River receded only after the leaders stepped into the rushing current in obedience and faith. *"As soon as the priests who carried the ark reached the Jordan and their feet touched the water's edge, the water from upstream stopped flowing . . . The whole nation completed the crossing on dry ground"* (Joshua 3:15-17 NIV).

What should you do when you know something is God's will but you're scared to death to do it? Do it anyway. Faith is about taking the first step. God waits for you to act first. Don't wait to feel powerful or confident. Move ahead in your weakness. Do the right thing in spite of your fears and feelings. The Bible says, *"For our life is a matter of faith, not of sight"* (2 Corinthians 5:7 TEV). This is how you cooperate with the Holy Spirit.

Obedience unlocks God's power. Daring faith is the key to miracles.

WHAT DID YOU HEAR?

What did God say to you as you read today's Scripture and devotion?

_____

_____

_____

WHAT DO YOU THINK?

How does it apply to your life?

_____

_____

_____

WHAT WILL YOU DO?

Don't just be a hearer of the word. Be a doer of the word. (James 1:22)

_____

_____

_____

NOW TALK TO GOD

This is where you turn your thoughts into prayer. It could be a prayer of gratitude or praise. It could be a prayer of confession or a request for God's help. It's up to you. Take a minute to write a prayer of response to what God said to you.

_____

_____

_____

_____

DAILY DEVOTIONS: DAY TWENTY
LISTEN TO GOD, NOT TO YOUR DOUBTS

"It was by faith that Noah built a large boat to save his family from the flood. He obeyed God, who warned him about things that had never happened before."
HEBREWS 11:7 (NLT)

The moment you take a step of faith related to your finances, family, career, or spiritual growth—the moment you set any kind of goal—there will be people who say, "Who do you think you are? It can't be done, forget about it!" They might be critics and cynics in the community. They might even be your friends and family. But the biggest doubts will come from the way you talk to yourself. You are the most influential doubter in your life. The question is whose voice are you going to listen to?

Faith means listening to God's voice and not the voices of doubt, no matter who they belong to.

Just imagine all the doubters in Noah's life. How would you like to be Noah's next-door neighbor? "That guy Noah, he thinks God speaks to him, but he's just ruining all of our property values by building that boat in his front yard." And imagine the pressure Noah got from his own family: "Why can't you just get a normal job? Everybody thinks we're weird!"

The Bible tells us that Noah listened to God. And what did he hear? *"God warned him about things that had never happened before"* (Hebrews 11:7 NLT), things that no one had ever seen or imagined. There had never been a flood. In fact, there had never even been rain. The Bible tells us the earth was watered by a mist that came up from the ground (Genesis 2:6).

Noah could have easily doubted himself. He could have dismissed God's voice as a bad pizza from the night before. He could have second guessed God's instructions: "I'm not so sure about this flood. But maybe I'll invent the umbrella, just in case."

Noah didn't listen to the voices of doubt from without or within. In faith, Noah followed God's instructions.

Has God told you to do something you have never done before? Do what Noah did. Step out in faith. Listen to God, not to your doubts.

WHAT DID YOU HEAR?

What did God say to you as you read today's Scripture and devotion?

_____

_____

_____

WHAT DO YOU THINK?

How does it apply to your life?

_____

_____

_____

WHAT WILL YOU DO?

Don't just be a hearer of the word. Be a doer of the word. (James 1:22)

_____

_____

_____

NOW TALK TO GOD

This is where you turn your thoughts into prayer. It could be a prayer of gratitude or praise. It could be a prayer of confession or a request for God's help. It's up to you. Take a minute to write a prayer of response to what God said to you.

_____

_____

_____

_____

DAILY DEVOTIONS: DAY TWENTY-ONE
WHEN GOD IS NEAR, YOU LOSE YOUR FEAR

*"Noah was a righteous man . . . he walked in close
fellowship with God."*
GENESIS 6:9 (NLT)

Noah built the ark in faith. *"He obeyed God, who warned him about things
that had never happened before"* (Hebrews 11:7 NLT). How could Noah believe
the things that had never happened before would actually take place? He
believed because he knew how to hear from God.

Do you want to hear from God? You can't hear God with the TV on. You can't
hear God when you are listening to your iPod or the radio. You can't hear God
when your mind is filled with a thousand distractions. You have to get alone
with God and be quiet. The Bible says, *"Be still, and know that I am God!"*
(Psalm 46:10 NIV).

Just sit quietly with your Bible, and pray, "God, is there anything you want to
say to me?" Then read God's Word and talk to him about what's on your heart.

You hear God by getting near God. The Bible calls this "walking in close
fellowship with God" (Genesis 6:9). When you walk with God you must go in
his direction and at his pace, not your own.

What is the result of walking with God? You fear nothing. The Psalmist said,
*"The Lord is my shepherd . . . Even though I walk through the valley of the
shadow of death, I will fear no evil"* (Psalm 23:4 NIV). Why does he fear
no evil? Because the Shepherd is leading him. When God is near, you lose
your fear.

Are you fearful about your future or your finances? Are you fearful about your
marriage or your health? *"Draw near to God and he will draw near to you"*
(James 4:8 NKJV). The more your life is filled with the love of God, the less
fear you will have in your life. Love and fear cannot operate in the same heart
at the same time. *"Perfect love casts out fear"* (1 John 4:18 NKJV).

WHAT DID YOU HEAR?

What did God say to you as you read today's Scripture and devotion?

_____

_____

_____

WHAT DO YOU THINK?

How does it apply to your life?

_____

_____

_____

WHAT WILL YOU DO?

Don't just be a hearer of the word. Be a doer of the word. (James 1:22)

_____

_____

_____

NOW TALK TO GOD

This is where you turn your thoughts into prayer. It could be a prayer of gratitude or praise. It could be a prayer of confession or a request for God's help. It's up to you. Take a minute to write a prayer of response to what God said to you.

_____

_____

_____

_____

TAKING THE INITIATIVE

CHECKING IN

- We're halfway through this study of *Daring Faith*. What is the most meaningful lesson you have learned in our study so far?

- Share a verse or insight that was especially meaningful to you in your *Daring Faith* daily devotions this past week.

MEMORY VERSE

"I can do all things through Christ who strengthens me."
PHILIPPIANS 4:13 (NKJV)

WATCH THE VIDEO LESSON NOW AND FOLLOW ALONG IN YOUR OUTLINE.

🌊 TAKING THE INITIATIVE

Have you been waiting for God to do something in your life? Maybe God is waiting for you to do something first.

> *"Show me your faith without doing anything, and I'll show you my faith by what I do . . . Faith that does nothing is worth nothing."*
> **JAMES 2:18-20 (NCV)**

When you take the initiative and step out in faith, you can hold on to God's promise that he will give you the strength to do what he is asking you to do.

- **Obey God** _____.

  If there is ever a time that you really ought to be in a hurry it's when God tells you to do something, whether you feel like it or not.

  "I will quickly obey your commands." **PSALM 119:32 (NCV)**

  "Without delay I hurry to obey your commands." **PSALM 119:60 (TEV)**

  What are you pretending God isn't telling you to do? If you want the blessing of God on your life, you must take the initiative and obey God immediately. Delayed obedience is disobedience.

- **Obey God** _____.

  Partial obedience is disobedience.

  "Lord, you gave your orders to be obeyed completely." **PSALM 119:4 (NCV)**

"Your job is not to decide whether God's law is right or wrong, but to obey it." JAMES 4:11 (TLB)

The oldest temptation is not lust, lying, or gluttony. It is the temptation to doubt God's word. Every sin starts with doubt.

"Trust God from the bottom of your heart; don't try to figure out everything on your own." PROVERBS 3:5 (MSG)

- **Obey God** _____.

  "Obey him gladly." PSALM 100:2 (TLB)

  "I enjoy obeying your commands." PSALM 119:47 (NCV)

  "Loving God means doing what he tells us to do." 1 JOHN 5:3 (TLB)

  God measures your love by your obedience.

  "If you love me, obey my commandments." JOHN 14:15 (NLT)

- **Obey God** _____.

  "I am determined to obey you until I die." PSALM 119:112 (TLB)

"Just tell me what to do and I'll do it, Lord. As long as I live I'll wholeheartedly obey." PSALM 119:33 (TLB)

"We must be sure to obey the truth we have learned already." PHILIPPIANS 3:16 (NLT)

If you are waiting for God to give you direction, and it's just not coming, ask him this question: "Lord, what have you already told me to do that I am not doing?"

Faith is like a muscle. It only grows when you exercise it by taking the initiative and stepping forward.

DISCOVERY QUESTIONS

- Review the four points of Pastor Rick's message. Which one do you need to work on most?

  - Obey God immediately, without delay, argument, or excuse.

  - Obey God completely, not picking and choosing the parts you like.

  - Obey God joyfully, with a pleasant attitude.

  - Obey God continually, not on and off or only when you feel like it.

- Before we look forward, let's look back: Has God already told you to do something that you are not doing? For example, do you need to get baptized? Do you need to begin tithing? Do you need to begin a daily quiet time with God? Do you need to forgive somebody or ask forgiveness? What is it for you? Two or three of you share with your group the step of obedience you need to take.

- Now let's look ahead: As you have prayed about stretching your imagination and getting God's dream for your life, what step of faith do you think God wants you to take? For example, are you facing a career decision? Do you need to share your faith with a lost friend or loved one? Is God is telling you to get involved in a ministry or an outreach at church? What does daring faith look like for you? Two or three of you share with the group what you believe God is asking you to do.

LIVING ON PURPOSE

- **Ministry:** Take an inventory of the gifts and abilities God has given you. How could they be used to serve others in your church or community? Ask God if there is something he wants you to do for him, and then take the initiative to act on it this week. What will be your first step? Take a few minutes to discuss this with your group, then give it more thought in your quiet time tomorrow.

PRAYER DIRECTION

- Begin your prayer time by reading the following verses aloud as a group:

  "Just tell me what to do and I'll do it, Lord. As long as I live, I'll wholeheartedly obey." PSALM 119:33

  "I can do all things through Christ who strengthens me." PHILIPPIANS 4:13

- Pray for each other to take the steps of obedience and initiative that God is calling you to do.

- Pray for each other's prayer requests. Be sure to record them on the *Small Group Prayer and Praise Report* on page 151 of this study guide. Commit to pray for each other's requests every day this week.

DIVING DEEPER

- Read the *Daring Faith* daily devotions for days 22-28 in this study guide. Write your thoughts and prayers on the journal pages. If it's more convenient, you can also listen to the daily devotions at **www.drivetimedevotions.com**. They're free!

- Read the Memory Verse on page 77 every day this week as part of your quiet time. See if you can memorize it before your next group meeting.

DARING FAITH INSTAGRAM CHALLENGE

- We dare you to share what a step of daring faith looks like for you. **#DaringFaith**

NOTES

DAILY DEVOTIONS: DAY TWENTY-TWO
DARING FAITH IS GENEROUS

"The generous will prosper; those who refresh others will themselves be refreshed."
PROVERBS 11:25 (NLT)

People with daring faith are generous even when they don't have anything to give. Anybody can be generous when they have a surplus. I can be generous with my time when I have extra time. I can be generous with my money when I have extra money. I can be generous with my energy when I have extra energy to spend. It's when I don't have enough time for me, enough money for me, or enough energy for me that God says, "This is a test. I'm watching you to see if you are faithful. Will you be generous, and will you trust me? Will you take me at my word when I promise, *'The generous will prosper; those who refresh others will themselves be refreshed'*" (Proverbs 11:25 NLT)?

Here are five principles in which God will test you and then bless you:

God gives to generous people. Why does God want you to be generous? Because he wants you to be like him, and God is a giver.

Obeying God's vision will bring God's provision. If you do what God tells you to do, God will bring along the resources you need at the right time. When he gives you the vision he will give you the *pro*vision.

When you do all that God tells you to do, he does what you can't do. God often asks you to do the impossible to stretch your faith. When you give what little you have, God multiplies it and makes up for what is lacking.

When you have a need, sow a seed. Whatever you need in your life, sow it as a seed, and it will come back to you.

There is always a delay between sowing and reaping. There is a season between planting and harvesting. What's going on in the delay? It's a test of your faith. Will you be faithful to give when you have little? Will you keep on doing the right thing? Do what God wants you to do, no matter the cost, and then see what God does.

WHAT DID YOU HEAR?

What did God say to you as you read today's Scripture and devotion?

_____

_____

_____

WHAT DO YOU THINK?

How does it apply to your life?

_____

_____

_____

WHAT WILL YOU DO?

Don't just be a hearer of the word. Be a doer of the word. (James 1:22)

_____

_____

_____

NOW TALK TO GOD

This is where you turn your thoughts into prayer. It could be a prayer of gratitude or praise. It could be a prayer of confession or a request for God's help. It's up to you. Take a minute to write a prayer of response to what God said to you.

_____

_____

_____

_____

DAILY DEVOTIONS: DAY TWENTY-THREE

GIVE AND LIVE WITH AN ATTITUDE OF GRATITUDE

"You will be made rich in every way so that you can be generous on every occasion . . . your generosity will result in thanksgiving to God."

2 CORINTHIANS 9:11 (NIV)

What an amazing promise! God makes you rich in every way so you can be generous on every occasion, which will result in thanksgiving to God. You give because you're grateful, and your gift makes others grateful too.

God doesn't bless you so you can be greedy. He blesses you so you can be generous. He gives to you so that he can give through you. He wants you to experience the blessing of generosity. Jesus said, *"More blessings come from giving than from receiving"* (Acts 20:35 CEV).

When you give, God gives back to you so that you can give more away, and he can give more back to you, and on and on and on. God doesn't give you things so you can pile them up. He wants you to be a river, not a reservoir. When you let go of what's in your hand, your hand is now ready to receive greater blessings from God.

God gives to you based on your attitude. That's why it's so important to live with an attitude of gratitude. The Bible says, *"This service that you perform is not only supplying the needs of God's people but is also overflowing in many expressions of thanks to God"* (2 Corinthians 9:12 NIV). When you give, you are performing a service. When you give, you are God's source of blessing to someone else.

To serve and to give are the same thing. They are expressions of love to God and to people. You can serve without loving, but you can't love without serving. You can give without loving, but you can't love without giving.

WHAT DID YOU HEAR?

What did God say to you as you read today's Scripture and devotion?

WHAT DO YOU THINK?

How does it apply to your life?

WHAT WILL YOU DO?

Don't just be a hearer of the word. Be a doer of the word. (James 1:22)

NOW TALK TO GOD

This is where you turn your thoughts into prayer. It could be a prayer of gratitude or praise. It could be a prayer of confession or a request for God's help. It's up to you. Take a minute to write a prayer of response to what God said to you.

DAILY DEVOTIONS: DAY TWENTY-FOUR
GOD IS WAITING FOR YOU TO PLANT A SEED

"Unless a kernel of wheat falls to the ground and dies, it remains only a single seed. But if it dies, it produces many seeds."
JOHN 12:24 (NIV)

What does a farmer do with a barren field that's producing no income? He doesn't complain about it. He doesn't worry about it. He doesn't even need to pray about it. He just goes out and plants some seed. He knows that nothing is going to grow until the seed is in the ground.

Everything in life starts as a seed—a life, a relationship, a business, even a church. And nothing happens until the seed is planted.

Are you waiting on God for a windfall? God says, "I'm waiting for you to plant a seed." Why does God require us to plant a seed? Because sowing seed is an act of faith. Planting is participating with God's process of fruitfulness. When you sow seed, you take what you have and give it away. That takes faith! And it brings glory to God.

Jesus described this principle of sowing and reaping when he explained why he came to earth to die on the cross. Jesus said, *"Unless a kernel of wheat falls to the ground and dies, it remains only a single seed. But if it dies, it produces many seeds"* (John 12:24 NIV). Jesus was saying, "Millions of people will be saved and go to heaven because of my death and resurrection. I'm going to plant a seed, and the seed is my life."

Here is the principle of sowing and reaping: Whatever you need, plant a seed. If you need more time, give more time to your kids. If you need more money, give more money to someone who needs it. If you need more wisdom, share the wisdom you have with others. Whatever you need, plant a seed. Give yourself away!

It may not make sense to give away something that you need more of, but that is exactly the attitude that God wants to bless, and it will produce fruit in your life. When you have a need, don't gripe about it, don't wish about it, don't worry about it—just plant a seed!

WHAT DID YOU HEAR?

What did God say to you as you read today's Scripture and devotion?

_____

_____

_____

WHAT DO YOU THINK?

How does it apply to your life?

_____

_____

_____

WHAT WILL YOU DO?

Don't just be a hearer of the word. Be a doer of the word. (James 1:22)

_____

_____

_____

NOW TALK TO GOD

This is where you turn your thoughts into prayer. It could be a prayer of gratitude or praise. It could be a prayer of confession or a request for God's help. It's up to you. Take a minute to write a prayer of response to what God said to you.

_____

_____

_____

_____

DAILY DEVOTIONS: DAY TWENTY-FIVE
PLANT TODAY, THEN BE PATIENT FOR THE HARVEST

*"Those who plant in tears will harvest with shouts of joy.
They weep as they go to plant their seed, but they sing as
they return with the harvest."*
PSALM 126:5-6 (NLT)

The time to start planting is now. I talk to people all the time who say, "One of these days, I'm going to . . ." They're going to serve more when they retire. They're going to give more when they get a raise. Whatever it is they're going to do more of, they're going do it "one of these days." But "one of these days" becomes none of these days.

Don't wait for things to get better; start planting seeds now. Why? Because the sooner you plant, the sooner you will enjoy the harvest.

But the harvest will not come according to your timetable. There's always a delay between sowing and reaping. You plant in one season, and harvest in another. You have to be patient and not give up! The Bible says, *"Let us not become tired of doing good; for if we do not give up, the time will come when we will reap the harvest"* (Galatians 6:9 TEV). The results will come, but they will come slowly and as part of a process.

What should you do in the meantime? Forget about last year's crop failure. Instead, focus on the long-term harvest in your life.

What loss have you been grieving over? Maybe you've lost a loved one. Maybe you've lost your health. Maybe you've lost your job, or your savings, or your retirement. Maybe you've lost your dream. Mourning is ok; moaning is not. Instead of moaning, you need to plant a seed, because nothing grows until a seed is planted. Whatever you need more of, you need to give away. Don't wait for "one of these days." Today is the day to plant the seed. The Bible says, *"Those who plant in tears will harvest with shouts of joy. They weep as they go to plant their seed, but they sing as they return with the harvest"* (Psalm 126:5-6 NLT).

WHAT DID YOU HEAR?

What did God say to you as you read today's Scripture and devotion?

_____

_____

_____

WHAT DO YOU THINK?

How does it apply to your life?

_____

_____

_____

WHAT WILL YOU DO?

Don't just be a hearer of the word. Be a doer of the word. (James 1:22)

_____

_____

_____

NOW TALK TO GOD

This is where you turn your thoughts into prayer. It could be a prayer of gratitude or praise. It could be a prayer of confession or a request for God's help. It's up to you. Take a minute to write a prayer of response to what God said to you.

_____

_____

_____

_____

DAILY DEVOTIONS: DAY TWENTY-SIX
SHOW YOUR FAITH THROUGH GENEROSITY

"Be generous: Invest in acts of charity. Charity yields high returns. Don't hoard your goods; spread them around. Be a blessing to others."
ECCLESIASTES 11:1-2 (MSG)

God wants you to use some of your money to help people in need. God didn't put you on this earth to live for yourself. He blesses you so that you can bless others. This is all part of God making you more like himself.

Everything you have in life is because of God's generosity. You wouldn't have anything—you wouldn't even be alive—if it weren't for God's generosity. Even your ability to create wealth is a gift from God. *"Remember the Lord your God, for it is he who gives you the ability to produce wealth"* (Deuteronomy 8:18 NIV). God is generous, and he wants you to be generous like he is.

Imagine your father is a billionaire, and he wants to share his fortune with you. But he knows you need to be tested first to see if you will be able to handle it. So he gives you a set amount of money and says, "I want you to learn to live on less so you can use the rest to help others. I'm going to be watching you to see how you manage and distribute my resources. If you do well, I'm going to will it all to you." How will you use that money?

God especially wants you to be generous with the poor. Throughout the Bible, God tells us he is watching how we help the poor, and he attaches tremendous promises if we do so. For example: *"Give to the poor and you will never be in need. If you close your eyes to the poor, many will curse you"* (Proverbs 28:27 TEV). *"When you give to the poor, it is like lending to the Lord, and the Lord will pay you back"* (Proverbs 19:17 TEV).

You are blessed to be a blessing. The more you help others, the more God blesses you. He gives to you so you can give to others. Why? Because God wants you to be like him, and God is a giver!

WHAT DID YOU HEAR?

What did God say to you as you read today's Scripture and devotion?

_____

_____

_____

WHAT DO YOU THINK?

How does it apply to your life?

_____

_____

_____

WHAT WILL YOU DO?

Don't just be a hearer of the word. Be a doer of the word. (James 1:22)

_____

_____

_____

NOW TALK TO GOD

This is where you turn your thoughts into prayer. It could be a prayer of gratitude or praise. It could be a prayer of confession or a request for God's help. It's up to you. Take a minute to write a prayer of response to what God said to you.

_____

_____

_____

_____

DAILY DEVOTIONS: DAY TWENTY-SEVEN
THE BEST FINANCIAL INVESTMENT YOU CAN MAKE

"Tell them to use their money to do good. They should be rich in good works and generous to those in need, always being ready to share with others. By doing this they will be storing up their treasure as a good foundation for the future so that they may experience true life."
1 TIMOTHY 6:18-19 (NLT)

Jesus told us to store up our treasures in heaven (Matthew 6:20-21). How can we do this? In one of his most misunderstood statements, Jesus said, *"I tell you, use worldly wealth to gain friends for yourselves, so that when it is gone, you will be welcomed into eternal dwellings"* (Luke 16:9 NIV).

Jesus did not mean for you to "buy" friends with money. What he meant was that you should use the money God gives you to bring people to Christ.

You've probably heard the expression, "You can't take it with you." But the Bible says you can send it on ahead. How? By investing in people who are going there. They will be friends for eternity who will welcome you when you get to heaven. It's the best financial investment you'll ever make! Imagine being greeted in heaven by someone who says, "I'm here because you gave the time, the money, and the effort to help me hear the gospel. If it weren't for you, I might not be here." Is anybody going to be in heaven because of you?

When you use your money to buy a Bible for somebody who doesn't have one, you are storing up treasure in heaven. When you use your money to share the Good News around the world, you are storing up treasure in heaven. When you use your money to help build a church, you are storing up treasure in heaven. That is the highest and best use of your money, and the return on your investment will be endlessly rewarding. *"By doing this [you] will be storing up real treasure for [yourself] in heaven—it is the only safe investment for eternity! And [you] will be living a fruitful Christian life down here as well"* (1 Timothy 6:19 TLB).

WHAT DID YOU HEAR?

What did God say to you as you read today's Scripture and devotion?

_____

_____

_____

WHAT DO YOU THINK?

How does it apply to your life?

_____

_____

_____

WHAT WILL YOU DO?

Don't just be a hearer of the word. Be a doer of the word. (James 1:22)

_____

_____

_____

NOW TALK TO GOD

This is where you turn your thoughts into prayer. It could be a prayer of gratitude or praise. It could be a prayer of confession or a request for God's help. It's up to you. Take a minute to write a prayer of response to what God said to you.

_____

_____

_____

_____

DAILY DEVOTIONS: DAY TWENTY-EIGHT
THE PROMISE, PURPOSE, PLACE, AND DAY FOR TITHING

"The purpose of tithing is to teach you always
to put God first in your lives."
DEUTERONOMY 14:23 (TLB)

Give God first place in whatever you want him to bless. If you want God to bless your home, put him first in your home. If you want God to bless your business, put him first in your business. If you want God to bless your finances, put him first in your finances.

The word tithe means ten percent. Tithing is giving the first ten percent of your income back to God. Here are four verses that explain the promise, the purpose, the place, and the day for tithing.

The Promise: *"Honor the Lord by giving him the first part of all your income, and he will fill your barns with wheat and barley and overflow your wine vats with the finest wines"* (Proverbs 3:9-10 TLB). God promises that if you honor him with the first part of your income, he will bless you financially.

The Purpose: *"The purpose of tithing is to teach you always to put God first in your lives"* (Deuteronomy 14:23 TLB). God doesn't need your money, but he wants what it represents—your heart. He wants you to trust him.

The Place: *"'Bring to the storehouse a full tenth of what you earn . . . Test me in this,' says the Lord All-Powerful. 'I will open the windows of heaven for you and pour out all the blessings you need'"* (Malachi 3:10 NCV). The storehouse is the place where you worship God. Giving to a relief organization or to someone in need is charity, but it is not tithing. Tithing is an act of worship, given at the place of worship.

The Day: *"On every Lord's Day each of you should put aside something from what you have earned during the week, and use it for this offering"* (1 Corinthians 16:2 TLB). When are you supposed to tithe? You tithe on the day you worship. By giving God the first part of your income on the first day of the week, you are saying to him, "You are number one in my life." Then watch how God blesses and uses you, and honors his promise in your life.

WHAT DID YOU HEAR?

What did God say to you as you read today's Scripture and devotion?

_____

_____

_____

WHAT DO YOU THINK?

How does it apply to your life?

_____

_____

_____

WHAT WILL YOU DO?

Don't just be a hearer of the word. Be a doer of the word. (James 1:22)

_____

_____

_____

NOW TALK TO GOD

This is where you turn your thoughts into prayer. It could be a prayer of gratitude or praise. It could be a prayer of confession or a request for God's help. It's up to you. Take a minute to write a prayer of response to what God said to you.

_____

_____

_____

_____

FACING YOUR FEARS

⊛ CHECKING IN

- In the Living on Purpose section of session four, you were encouraged to take a step toward getting involved in a ministry at the church or an outreach in the community. Does anyone have a follow-up story to share?

- Share a verse or insight that was especially meaningful to you in your *Daring Faith* daily devotions this past week.

⊛ MEMORY VERSE

"With God's power working in us, God can do much, much more than anything we can ask or imagine." **EPHESIANS 3:20 (NCV)**

⊛ WATCH THE VIDEO LESSON NOW AND FOLLOW ALONG IN YOUR OUTLINE.

☸ FACING YOUR FEARS

Life is all about taking risks. How do you take risks in faith rather than caving in to fear?

- **The Principle of _____: Get the Facts.**

   "Every prudent man acts out of knowledge." PROVERBS 13:16 (NIV)

   Wise people think before they act. They do all they can to fully understand the risk they are about to take.

   "Get the facts at any price." PROVERBS 23:23 (TLB)

   The facts may be scary, but there is nothing more frightening than ignorance.

- **The Principle of _____: Count the Cost.**

   "Don't begin until you count the cost. For who would begin construction of a building without first getting estimates . . . Or what king would dream of going to war without first sitting down with his counselors and discussing whether his army of 10,000 is strong enough to defeat the 20,000 men who are marching against him?" LUKE 14:28-31 (TLB)

   Know what you have. Know what you need. Know what you are trusting God for. Every decision has a price tag.

- **The Principle of _____: Plan Your Steps.**

You have to think about what you are doing and where you are going. God gave you a brain because he meant for you to use it.

"A prudent man gives thought to his steps." PROVERBS 14:15 (NIV)

"We should make plans—counting on God to direct us."
PROVERBS 16:9 (TLB)

Prayer and preparation go together. As you pray, plan. And as you plan, pray, asking God to direct you. The prepared life is an effective life.

- **The principle of _____: Announce Your Goal.**

"What you should say is this, 'If the Lord is willing, we will live and do this or that.'" JAMES 4:15 (TEV)

Goals are statements of faith. When you announce your goal it builds your faith and holds you accountable to other people.

- **The Principle of _____: Let Go and Leap Out.**

"When I am afraid, I will put my confidence in you. Yes, I will trust the promises of God." PSALM 56:3 (TLB)

Courage is not the absence of fear. Courage is moving ahead in spite of your fear.

"I have the strength to face all conditions by the power that Christ gives me." PHILIPPIANS 4:13 (TEV)

- **The Key to Daring Faith:** _____
  _____.

"Then the Lord said to Moses, 'Quit praying and get the people moving! Forward, march!'" EXODUS 14:15 (TLB)

Can you imagine God saying such a thing? "Quit praying and get moving!" People often use prayer as an excuse to procrastinate. But there comes a time when you must stop talking about it and thinking about it and praying about it, and just do something about it.

DISCOVERY QUESTIONS

- Ephesians 3:20 (NCV) says, *"With God's power working in us, God can do much, much more than anything we can ask or imagine."* What are you asking? What are you imagining God can do in and through your life?

- Is there something you need to stop talking and thinking and praying about, and just start doing? What is your personal Red Sea?

- Pastor Rick said, "You have to move against your fear . . . Like the trapeze artist, it's time to let go and leap out." What fear do you need to move against? What practical step can you take to move in the right direction?

LIVING ON PURPOSE

- **Evangelism:** Jesus said, *"You will be my witnesses"* (Acts 1:8 NIV). A witness simply tells others what he has seen, heard, and experienced. Who do you know that needs to hear what have you seen, heard, and experienced in your walk with Christ? Share their name with your group. Are you afraid to share your faith with them? What could happen if you moved against your fear?

PRAYER DIRECTION

- Pray for each other that God will give you courage to move against your fears this week.

- Pray for each other's prayer requests. Be sure to record them on the *Small Group Prayer and Praise Report* on page 151 of this study guide. Commit to pray for each other's requests every day this week.

DIVING DEEPER

- Read the *Daring Faith* daily devotions for days 29-35 in this study guide. Write your thoughts and prayers on the journal pages. If it's more convenient, you can also listen to the daily devotions at **www.drivetimedevotions.com**. They're free!

- Read the Memory Verse on page 99 every day this week as part of your quiet time. See if you can memorize it before your next group meeting.

DARING FAITH INSTAGRAM CHALLENGE

- We dare you to share a picture of the people who will be supporting you as you move against your fears. **#DaringFaith**

BEFORE YOU GO

- There is only one session left in this study of Daring Faith. This would be a good time to decide what you want to study next in your small group. Visit **www.rickwarren.org**, to find more video-based small group studies.

- Plan a seventh session together where you can celebrate what God has done in your lives through this small group study. This should be a dinner, barbecue, or picnic where the focus is on fellowship. It is also an excellent opportunity to invite people who might be interested in joining your small group. Start making plans now.

NOTES

DAILY DEVOTIONS: DAY TWENTY-NINE
LOOK FOR GOD'S PROMISE TO MOVE FORWARD IN FAITH

"I've banked your promises in the vault of my heart."
PSALM 119:11 (MSG)

There are over seven thousand promises in the Bible. They're like blank checks, signed by God, waiting for you to cash. I hope you are memorizing each of the weekly memory verses in this study guide, because you need to get some of God's promises stored up in your mind and heart. When you start to doubt, when you start to feel discouraged or depressed, the Holy Spirit can bring these promises to your memory. The Bible says, *"I have banked your promises in the vault of my heart"* (Psalm 119:11 MSG).

When you tell God that you want to be used for his purposes, he promises you three things that are all found in Joshua chapter one.

- **God promises to give you strength:** *"No one will be able to stand against you"* (Joshua 1:5). In other words, when God asks you to do something, he will give you the power to do it. Where God guides, he provides.

- **God promises to give you success:** *"You will be successful"* (Joshua 1:7-8). God does not promise to make you successful at whatever you want to do; he promises you will be successful at what he wants you to do. If you want to be a success in life, it's real simple: start doing what God made you to do.

- **God promises to support you:** *"I will be with you wherever you go"* (Joshua 1:9 NIV). God's work done God's way will not lack God's support.

There are so many more promises for you in the Bible, but you have to discover them. The Bible says, *"Always remember what is written in [this book]. Study it day and night to be sure to obey everything that is written there. If you do this, you will be wise and successful in everything"* (Joshua 1:8 NCV). That's quite a promise!

WHAT DID YOU HEAR?

What did God say to you as you read today's Scripture and devotion?

_____

_____

_____

WHAT DO YOU THINK?

How does it apply to your life?

_____

_____

_____

WHAT WILL YOU DO?

Don't just be a hearer of the word. Be a doer of the word. (James 1:22)

_____

_____

_____

NOW TALK TO GOD

This is where you turn your thoughts into prayer. It could be a prayer of gratitude or praise. It could be a prayer of confession or a request for God's help. It's up to you. Take a minute to write a prayer of response to what God said to you.

_____

_____

_____

_____

DAILY DEVOTIONS: DAY THIRTY
REPLACE YOUR FEARS WITH FAITH

"From such terrible dangers of death he saved us, and will save us; and we have placed our hope in him that he will save us again."

2 CORINTHIANS 1:10 (TEV)

Fear is a choice. God is watching over you. He knows everything you are going through, and he is not afraid of the outcome of any hardship or trial you are facing. If God is not afraid, you don't have to be afraid either. Trust God, and don't give in to your fears.

When the Apostle Paul was facing certain death, he said, *"This happened so that we should rely, not on ourselves, but only on God, who raises the dead. From such terrible dangers of death he saved us, and will save us; and we have placed our hope in him that he will save us again"* (2 Corinthians 1:9-10 TEV). Paul had the right perspective. He made the right choice. He replaced his fears with faith.

God's promise to believers is that, no matter what happens, *"in all things God works for the good of those who love him"* (Romans 8:28 NIV). It doesn't say *all things are good*, but that they are *working together* for good.

That means you can stop listening to your fears. There is no difficulty, dilemma, defeat, or disaster in your life that God cannot ultimately use for your good and for his glory. There is no need to fear the future.

Your fears reveal where you do not trust God. Today, make a list of your fears, and ask God to help you identify why you have fear in those areas. Then ask him to help you replace your fears with faith.

WHAT DID YOU HEAR?

What did God say to you as you read today's Scripture and devotion?

_____

_____

_____

WHAT DO YOU THINK?

How does it apply to your life?

_____

_____

_____

WHAT WILL YOU DO?

Don't just be a hearer of the word. Be a doer of the word. (James 1:22)

_____

_____

_____

NOW TALK TO GOD

This is where you turn your thoughts into prayer. It could be a prayer of gratitude or praise. It could be a prayer of confession or a request for God's help. It's up to you. Take a minute to write a prayer of response to what God said to you.

_____

_____

_____

_____

DAILY DEVOTIONS: DAY THIRTY-ONE
FAITH IS MORE THAN BELIEVING:
TAKE THE NEXT STEP

"And Jesus said to him, 'Go; your faith has made you well.' Immediately he regained his sight and began following him on the road."
MARK 10:52 (NASB)

I don't know what your next step of faith is, but I do know this: You have one. God will never be finished taking you deeper in faith. There is always a next step.

If you don't take the next step, you'll get stuck in a rut—and the only difference between a grave and a rut is the length. If you don't move forward in faith, your heart will grow cold, and you will feel more distant from God. He isn't going to help you with step three, four, and five until you take step one. If you're asking God to help you with something, he's asking *you*, "Why haven't you done what I've already told you to do?" You may have "been aiming to" do something. Stop aiming and pull the trigger.

In Mark chapter ten, Jesus healed a blind man named Bartimaeus. Before Bartimaeus met Jesus, he was sitting beside the road. After he received his sight from the Lord, he *"began following him on the road"* (Mark 10:52b NASB). Which of those two phrases describes your life: sitting beside the road or following Jesus on the road?

There is only one way to follow Jesus on the road: Take the next step.

Faith is more than believing. Faith is more than thinking, talking, or having convictions about Jesus. Faith is action. It is movement. It is activity. Faith is something you do. In fact, the Bible says, *"If people say they have faith, but do nothing, their faith is worth nothing"* (James 2:14 NCV).

What "next step" will you take today to move forward in faith?

WHAT DID YOU HEAR?

What did God say to you as you read today's Scripture and devotion?

_____

_____

_____

WHAT DO YOU THINK?

How does it apply to your life?

_____

_____

_____

WHAT WILL YOU DO?

Don't just be a hearer of the word. Be a doer of the word. (James 1:22)

_____

_____

_____

NOW TALK TO GOD

This is where you turn your thoughts into prayer. It could be a prayer of gratitude or praise. It could be a prayer of confession or a request for God's help. It's up to you. Take a minute to write a prayer of response to what God said to you.

_____

_____

_____

_____

DAILY DEVOTIONS: DAY THIRTY-TWO
DARE TO SELL OUT

"The eyes of the Lord search the whole earth in order to strengthen those whose hearts are fully committed to him."

2 CHRONICLES 16:9 (NLT)

The Bible tells us three things about the importance of daring faith.

- **God is looking for faithful people.** God is actively searching for people who are sold out to his purposes, so that he can bless them. The Bible says, *"The eyes of the Lord search the whole earth in order to strengthen those whose hearts are fully committed to him"* (2 Chronicles 16:9 NLT). This has been one of my life verses. I've learned that if you make yourself usable, God will wear you out. If you get bless-able, he will bless your socks off! God is looking for faithful people that he can use.

- **Faithful people are hard to find.** The Bible says, *"Everyone talks about how faithful he is, but just try to find someone who really is!"* (Proverbs 20:6 TEV). A lot of people talk the talk. They say they believe in God, but when things get tough in their finances, or their health, or their job, instead of seeking God, they doubt God—or they blame him for their troubles. The Bible says, *"God looks down from heaven on the entire human race; he looks to see if anyone is truly wise, if anyone seeks God."* (Psalm 53:2 NLT).

- **Faithfulness is the key to blessing and victory.** The Bible says, *"A faithful man will have many blessings"* (Proverbs 28:20 HCSB). I want your life to have many blessings. But in order for you to be blessed, you have to learn faithfulness.

  The Bible says, *"Every child of God defeats this evil world, and we achieve this victory through our faith. And who can win this battle against the world? Only those who believe that Jesus is the Son of God"* (1 John 5:4-5 NLT).

If you stay faithful to the Lord, he will strengthen your heart and use your life for his purposes.

WHAT DID YOU HEAR?

What did God say to you as you read today's Scripture and devotion?

_____

_____

_____

WHAT DO YOU THINK?

How does it apply to your life?

_____

_____

_____

WHAT WILL YOU DO?

Don't just be a hearer of the word. Be a doer of the word. (James 1:22)

_____

_____

_____

NOW TALK TO GOD

This is where you turn your thoughts into prayer. It could be a prayer of gratitude or praise. It could be a prayer of confession or a request for God's help. It's up to you. Take a minute to write a prayer of response to what God said to you.

_____

_____

_____

_____

DAILY DEVOTIONS: DAY THIRTY-THREE
CHOOSE HOPE

"Yet hope returns when I remember this one thing: The Lord's unfailing love and mercy still continue, fresh as the morning, as sure as the sunrise. The Lord is all I have, and so in him I put my hope."
LAMENTATIONS 3:21-24 (TEV)

Pain is a natural part of life. We can't escape it. Broken relationships, missed opportunities, and rough seasons will always be with us. When they come, you can either become bitter or hopeful. The choice is yours.

Jeremiah faced the same choice. When his world came apart, the prophet wrote the book of Lamentations to share his honest frustrations with God. But he didn't settle in his bitterness. After sharing his bitter feelings, he wrote, *"Yet hope returns when I remember this one thing: The Lord's unfailing love and mercy still continue, fresh as the morning, as sure as the sunrise. The Lord is all I have, and so in him I put my hope"* (Lamentations 3:21-24 TEV). In the midst of a terrible situation, Jeremiah changed his perspective.

It's healthy and good to be honest with God about your feelings, but eventually you have to change your perspective. As long as your mind is on your pain, you won't solve anything. Instead, like Jeremiah, you need to recognize God's unfailing love and mercy for you. No matter what the problem, no matter how much anger you've spewed at God, he still loves you, and that will never change.

The longer you focus on what depresses you, the longer your depression will last. Bitterness keeps you caught in your own pain. Jeremiah gives us a simple cure for bitterness: In the midst of a depressing tirade, he says, *"Yet hope returns . . ."*

How can you have hope even in your darkest days? By remembering that *"the Lord's unfailing love and mercy still continue."* You can count on that! God's mercies are *"as fresh as the morning"* and *"as sure as the sunrise."* He is all you need. And, no matter what, you can put your hope in him.

You'll never know that God is all you need until he's all you have. Are you there yet? There's no better place to be.

WHAT DID YOU HEAR?

What did God say to you as you read today's Scripture and devotion?

_____

_____

_____

WHAT DO YOU THINK?

How does it apply to your life?

_____

_____

_____

WHAT WILL YOU DO?

Don't just be a hearer of the word. Be a doer of the word. (James 1:22)

_____

_____

_____

NOW TALK TO GOD

This is where you turn your thoughts into prayer. It could be a prayer of gratitude or praise. It could be a prayer of confession or a request for God's help. It's up to you. Take a minute to write a prayer of response to what God said to you.

_____

_____

_____

_____

DAILY DEVOTIONS: DAY THIRTY-FOUR
HOW TO SET A FAITH GOAL

"I know that I have not yet reached that goal, but there is one thing I always do. Forgetting the past and straining toward what is ahead, I keep trying to reach the goal and get the prize for which God called me through Christ to the life above."
PHILIPPIANS 3:13-14 (NCV)

You exercise faith by setting goals. Goals are statements of faith by which you say, "I believe God wants me to accomplish something by a certain date." If you don't have a date, it's not a goal, it's just a wish, a dream, a desire. Wishes are a dime a dozen. The only thing that will change your life is setting a goal. You have to wake up from the dream and go to work!

A "FAITH" goal has five characteristics:

Focused: That means it is specific. If you use the words "more" or "less," it's not a focused goal. "I want to be more like Jesus" or "I want to weigh less" are not goals because you can't measure them. A goal must be specific. For example, "I will have a quiet time for five minutes every day for the next month," or "I will lose ten pounds in thirty days—those are FAITH goals."

Attainable: It must be possible and practical. If you set an unrealistic goal, it's just going to discourage you. If you say, "I'm going to pray three hours a day," you're setting yourself up for failure. Set a goal that stretches you without breaking you, and then trust God to help you stretch.

Individual: That means it's personal. You cannot set goals for other people, because you can't control them. You can only set goals for yourself.

Trackable: Trackable goals can be measured and verified. Your goal needs a deadline. Without a date, it's not a goal.

Heartfelt: You'll never reach a passionless goal. If you don't have a deep desire to do it, don't set it.

Goals will give life to the dreams you've given up for dead. Take a look at the dreams you've given up on. Add a goal, and see what God can do.

WHAT DID YOU HEAR?

What did God say to you as you read today's Scripture and devotion?

_____

_____

_____

WHAT DO YOU THINK?

How does it apply to your life?

_____

_____

_____

WHAT WILL YOU DO?

Don't just be a hearer of the word. Be a doer of the word. (James 1:22)

_____

_____

_____

NOW TALK TO GOD

This is where you turn your thoughts into prayer. It could be a prayer of gratitude or praise. It could be a prayer of confession or a request for God's help. It's up to you. Take a minute to write a prayer of response to what God said to you.

_____

_____

_____

_____

DAILY DEVOTIONS: DAY THIRTY-FIVE
DARING FAITH HAS BIG DREAMS

"Now glory be to God, who by his mighty power at work within us is able to do far more than we would ever dare to ask or even dream of—infinitely beyond our highest prayers, desires, thoughts, or hopes."
EPHESIANS 3:20 (TLB)

Dreaming is an act of faith. God gave you the ability to create and to imagine, but nothing happens in your life until you start dreaming. So how do you get God's dream for your life? You do three things:

- **Dare to ask God for it.** The Bible says, *"Now glory be to God, who by his mighty power at work within us is able to do far more than we would ever dare to ask or even dream of—infinitely beyond our highest prayers, desires, thoughts, or hopes"* (Ephesians 3:20 TLB). If you want God's dream for your life, you must dare to ask him what he wants you to do. Then ask yourself, "What would I attempt for God if I knew I couldn't fail?" Let that expand your vision.

- **Believe God's promises.** The Bible says, *"I am the Lord, the God of all the peoples of the world. Is anything too hard for me?"* (Jeremiah 32:27 NLT). Never let an impossible situation intimidate you. Let it motivate you to pray more, believe more, trust more, experience more, learn more, and grow more. Faith always works in the realm of the impossible.

- **Dream big.** *"Ask of me, and I will make the nations your inheritance, the ends of the earth your possession"* (Psalm 2:8 NIV). Let the size of your God determine the size of your goal. You haven't really believed God until you've attempted something that can't be done in the power of the flesh. God's dream for you will be a perfect match for your God-given SHAPE: your spiritual gifts, heart, abilities, personality, and experiences. But it will be impossible to achieve without *"his mighty power at work within you."*

Dream great dreams for God. It's the first step in your walk of faith.

WHAT DID YOU HEAR?

What did God say to you as you read today's Scripture and devotion?

_____

_____

_____

WHAT DO YOU THINK?

How does it apply to your life?

_____

_____

_____

WHAT WILL YOU DO?

Don't just be a hearer of the word. Be a doer of the word. (James 1:22)

_____

_____

_____

NOW TALK TO GOD

This is where you turn your thoughts into prayer. It could be a prayer of gratitude or praise. It could be a prayer of confession or a request for God's help. It's up to you. Take a minute to write a prayer of response to what God said to you.

_____

_____

_____

_____

BELIEVING WHILE YOU'RE WAITING

CHECKING IN

- In session one, you rated the strength of your faith on a scale of 1-10. How would you rate your faith today?

- Share a verse or insight that was especially meaningful to you in your *Daring Faith* daily devotions this past week.

MEMORY VERSE

"With God everything is possible." MATTHEW 19:26 (NLT)

WATCH THE VIDEO LESSON NOW AND FOLLOW ALONG IN YOUR OUTLINE.

🌊 BELIEVING WHILE YOU'RE WAITING

Have you ever been in a hurry when God wasn't? One of the most difficult things to do in life is to sit in God's waiting room. When you worship an eternal God, sometimes it can feel like you're waiting for an eternity.

The Six Phases of Faith

- **Phase One:** _____

  "The Lord had said to Abram, 'Leave your country, your people and your father's household and go to the land I will show you. I will make you into a great nation.'" GENESIS 12:1-2 (NIV)

- **Phase Two:** _____

  "So Abram left, as the Lord had told him." GENESIS 12:4 (NIV)

  A dream without a decision is worthless.

- **Phase Three:** _____

  "Now Sarai, Abram's wife, had borne him no children." GENESIS 16:1 (NIV)

- **Phase Four:** _____

  "Will a son be born to a man a hundred years old? Will Sarah bear a child at the age of ninety?" GENESIS 17:17 (NIV)

- **Phase Five:** _____

"Take your son, your only son, Isaac, whom you love, and . . .
sacrifice him as a burnt offering." GENESIS 22:2 (NIV)

- **Phase Six:** _____

"'Abraham! Abraham! . . . Do not lay a hand on the boy. Do not do
anything to him. Now I know that you fear God, because you have
not withheld from me your son, your only son.' Abraham looked
up and there in a thicket he saw a ram caught by its horns. He went
over and took the ram and sacrificed it as a burnt offering instead of
his son. So Abraham called that place 'The Lord Will Provide.'"
GENESIS 22:11-14 (NIV)

How to Keep Believing While You're Waiting on God

- **Remember** _____.

The situation may be out of your control but it's not out of
God's control.

"Abraham believed [in] the God who gives life to the dead and who
creates something out of nothing." ROMANS 4:17 (NCV)

"Anything is possible if you have faith." MARK 9:23 (TLB)

"What is impossible with men is possible with God." LUKE 18:27 (NIV)

- **Rely on** _____.

"When hope was dead within him, [Abraham] went on hoping in faith, believing that he would become 'the father of many nations.' He relied on the word of God." ROMANS 4:18 (PH)

- **Recognize** _____.

"Without weakening in his faith, he [Abraham] faced the fact that his body was as good as dead . . . and that Sarah's womb was also dead. Yet he did not waver through unbelief." ROMANS 4:19-20 (NIV)

"Through faith he regarded the facts." ROMANS 4:19 (GW)

Faith is not ignoring reality or pretending a problem does not exist. Faith is facing a hopeless situation without being discouraged by it.

- **Rejoice** _____.

Joyfully expect God to act in your life, even if it's not the way you planned.

"Abraham never doubted. He believed God, for his faith and trust grew ever stronger, and he praised God for this blessing even before it happened. He was completely sure that God was well able to do anything he promised." ROMANS 4:20-21 (TLB)

Three Kinds of Deliverance

- _____ **deliverance.**

  In this type of deliverance God miraculously changes the situation.

- _____ **deliverance.**

  In this type of deliverance God doesn't change the circumstance, he changes you.

- _____ **deliverance.**

  If you have placed your faith in Jesus Christ, ultimately he will deliver you to heaven where there is no sorrow, no suffering, no sadness, and no pain. That is God's ultimate deliverance.

"We rejoice in the hope of the glory of God." ROMANS 5:2 (NIV)

"I am the way, the truth and the life. No one comes to the Father except through me." JOHN 14:6 (NIV)

Jesus can take a hopeless end and turn it into an endless hope. He may not deliver you in the way you think he should, but he will deliver you in the way he knows is best.

DISCOVERY QUESTIONS

- Pastor Rick said the first thing to do while you're waiting on God is to "remember what God can do." What miracles has God already done in your life? How has he answered your prayers in the past? What did you learn about God in the process? Share stories of God's faithfulness with your group.

- Which phase of faith are you in right now? What do you think God is trying to teach you through it, and how does he want you to respond?

- What is the most meaningful lesson you have learned through this study of *Daring Faith*? What difference will that lesson make in your life?

- How have the people in your group helped to strengthen your faith?

LIVING ON PURPOSE

- **Worship:** As the old hymn says, "Count your blessings." Remembering the things God has done in the past will build your faith for your current situation. Take ten minutes during your quiet time tomorrow and make a list of all the things God has done for you. Write them down. Then tell him thanks. You will be amazed by what it does for your faith.

PRAYER DIRECTION

- Before you pray for each other's requests, thank God for the lessons you have learned in this *Daring Faith* study.

- Pray for each other that God will help you in whichever phase of faith you are in.

- Pray for each other's prayer requests. Be sure to record them on the *Small Group Prayer and Praise Report* on page 151 of this study guide. Commit to pray for each other's requests every day this week.

DIVING DEEPER

- Read the *Daring Faith* daily devotions for days 36-40 in your work book. Write your thoughts and prayers on the journal pages. If it's more convenient, you can also listen to the daily devotions at **www.drivetimedevotions.com**. They're free!

- Read the Memory Verse on page 121 every day this week as part of your quiet time.

DARING FAITH INSTAGRAM CHALLENGE

- We dare you to share one of God's promises you're relying on. **#DaringFaith**

BEFORE YOU GO

- Sign up for Pastor Rick's Daily Hope devotional email at **www.rickwarren.org/devotional**. It's absolutely free!

- Pastor Rick would love to stay connected with you.
  Email: PastorRick@saddleback.com
  Facebook: Pastor Rick Warren
  Instagram: PastorRickWarren
  Twitter: @RickWarren
  LinkedIn: Rick Warren2
  Google+: Rick Warren

- Visit **www.rickwarren.org** to find more video-based small group studies.

- Congratulations on completing this study. It's time to plan a party! Pick a date, time, and location for your group to celebrate the work God has done in your lives over these last six weeks.

NOTES

NOTES

DAILY DEVOTIONS: DAY THIRTY-SIX
DECISION-MAKING IS A FAITH-BUILDING ACTIVITY

"But when you pray, you must believe and not doubt at all. Whoever doubts is like a wave in the sea that is driven and blown about by the wind. If you are like that, unable to make up your mind and undecided in all you do, you must not think that you will receive anything from the Lord."

JAMES 1:6-8 (TEV)

Nothing is going to happen to your dream until you wake up and put it into action. You have to make the decision: "I'm going to go for it!" For every ten dreamers in the world, there is only one decision maker. Most people have dreams but they never get to this step—making the decision to trust God and step out in faith. And then they wonder why their dreams are not fulfilled.

James says, *"But when you pray, you must believe and not doubt at all. Whoever doubts is like a wave in the sea that is driven and blown about by the wind. If you are like that, unable to make up your mind and undecided in all you do, you must not think that you will receive anything from the Lord"* (James 1:6-8 TEV).

Faith is a verb. It's active and not passive. Faith is not just something you believe, it's something you do. You have to make up your mind and step up your pace.

Decision making is a faith-building activity that requires two things:

- **You must decide to invest your time, money, reputation, and energy.** You lay it all on the line; you take the plunge. You say, "God, you've told me to do this and I'm going to be faithful to do it!"

- **You have to let go of security.** You cannot move forward in faith and hold onto the past at the same time. In other words, if you want to walk on water, you have to get out of the boat.

WHAT DID YOU HEAR?

What did God say to you as you read today's Scripture and devotion?

_____

_____

_____

WHAT DO YOU THINK?

How does it apply to your life?

_____

_____

_____

WHAT WILL YOU DO?

Don't just be a hearer of the word. Be a doer of the word. (James 1:22)

_____

_____

_____

NOW TALK TO GOD

This is where you turn your thoughts into prayer. It could be a prayer of gratitude or praise. It could be a prayer of confession or a request for God's help. It's up to you. Take a minute to write a prayer of response to what God said to you.

_____

_____

_____

_____

DAILY DEVOTIONS: DAY THIRTY-SEVEN
FAITH, NOT FEELINGS, PLEASES GOD

*"Naked I came from my mother's womb, and naked I
will depart. The Lord gave and the Lord has taken
away; may the name of the Lord be praised."*
JOB 1:21 (NIV)

When you are a baby Christian, God gives you a lot of confirming emotions,
and often answers the most immature, self-centered prayers—so you'll know he
exists. But as you grow in faith, he will wean you of these dependencies.

God wants you to sense his presence, but he's more concerned that you trust
him than that you feel him. Faith, not feelings, pleases God. The Bible says,
"Without faith it is impossible to please God" (Hebrews 11:6 NIV).

The situations that will stretch your faith most will be those times when
life falls apart and God seems nowhere to be found. This happened to Job.
On a single day he lost everything—his family, his business, his health, and
everything he owned. Most discouraging for Job was that for thirty-seven
chapters of the Bible, God said nothing!

How do you trust God when he is silent? How do you stay connected in a crisis
without communication? How do you praise God when you don't understand
what's happening in your life? How do you keep your eyes on Jesus when
they're full of tears? You do what Job did: *"He fell to the ground in worship
and said, 'Naked I came from my mother's womb, and naked I will depart.
The Lord gave and the Lord has taken away; may the name of the Lord be
praised'"* (Job 1:21 NIV).

Tell God exactly how you feel. Pour out your heart to God. Unload every
emotion that you're feeling. Job did this when he said, *"I can't be quiet! I am
angry and bitter. I have to speak"* (Job 7:11 TEV).

Never be afraid to tell God what's on your mind. He can handle your doubt,
anger, fear, grief, confusion, and questions. And he'll never stop loving you.

WHAT DID YOU HEAR?

What did God say to you as you read today's Scripture and devotion?

_____

_____

_____

WHAT DO YOU THINK?

How does it apply to your life?

_____

_____

_____

WHAT WILL YOU DO?

Don't just be a hearer of the word. Be a doer of the word. (James 1:22)

_____

_____

_____

NOW TALK TO GOD

This is where you turn your thoughts into prayer. It could be a prayer of gratitude or praise. It could be a prayer of confession or a request for God's help. It's up to you. Take a minute to write a prayer of response to what God said to you.

_____

_____

_____

_____

DAILY DEVOTIONS: DAY THIRTY-EIGHT
EVERY DIFFICULTY IS FOR YOUR DEVELOPMENT

"For our light and momentary troubles are achieving for us an eternal glory that far outweighs them all."
2 CORINTHIANS 4:17 (NIV)

When we go through difficulties in life, the first thing we try to do is blame somebody else. But it doesn't matter where your problem came from—God still has a purpose for it in your life. Even when you do something stupid, God can use it. Even when other people hurt you intentionally, he can use it. Even when the devil plans bad things for your life, God can bring good out of it.

God's purpose is greater than your problem and your pain. God has a plan! You need to look past the temporary pain and look instead at the long-term benefit in your life.

The Bible says, *"We can rejoice, too, when we run into problems and trials, for we know that . . . they help us learn to be patient. And patience develops strength of character in us and helps us trust God more each time we use it until finally our hope and faith are strong and steady"* (Romans 5:3-4 TLB).

What is the purpose of your problems and difficulties? God wants you to learn something. Every storm is a school. Every trial is a teacher. Every experience is an education. Every difficulty is for your development.

Most of us are slow learners. If you don't learn something the first time, God will bring it up again in your life. It will come back, because God is more interested in your character than he is in your comfort. He is more interested in making you like Christ than he is in making things easy for you.

You might be facing a major difficulty right now: an illness, a financial problem, or strain in a relationship. Does God have a message for you while you're going through your difficulty? Absolutely. God is saying to you, "Don't give up. Grow up." *"Let patience have its perfect work, that you may be perfect and complete, lacking nothing"* (James 1:4 NKJV).

WHAT DID YOU HEAR?

What did God say to you as you read today's Scripture and devotion?

_____

_____

_____

WHAT DO YOU THINK?

How does it apply to your life?

_____

_____

_____

WHAT WILL YOU DO?

Don't just be a hearer of the word. Be a doer of the word. (James 1:22)

_____

_____

_____

NOW TALK TO GOD

This is where you turn your thoughts into prayer. It could be a prayer of gratitude or praise. It could be a prayer of confession or a request for God's help. It's up to you. Take a minute to write a prayer of response to what God said to you.

_____

_____

_____

_____

DAILY DEVOTIONS: DAY THIRTY-NINE
GOD IS IN CONTROL IN YOUR DEAD END

"Abraham believed in the God who brings the dead back to life and who creates new things out of nothing."
ROMANS 4:17 (NLT)

There are certain dead-end words in life: cancer, divorce, bankruptcy, infertility, and unemployment, to name a few. How do you know when you're at a dead end? You know it when things get out of your control.

When you're at a dead end and you're waiting for deliverance, you need to remember this: The situation may be out of your control, but it's not out of God's control. When you face a dead end, don't focus on what you can't do. Focus instead on what God can do.

There are two things God can do that you can't do: He can *"bring the dead back to life and create new things out of nothing"* (Romans 4:17 NLT). If God can give life to a dead man, he can bring life to a dead career. He can bring life to a dead marriage. He can bring life to a dead dream. He can bring life to a financial dead end.

When you face things that are out of your control, you need something more than a positive mental attitude. You need faith in God, because he can control things when you can't. Most of life is beyond your control, so you need faith far more than you need positive thinking.

The Bible says, *"What is impossible with men is possible with God"* (Luke 18:27 NIV). God turns crucifixions into resurrections. He specializes in the impossible. It's called "miracles," and he can do one in your life! God is ready to turn your dead end into deliverance.

WHAT DID YOU HEAR?

What did God say to you as you read today's Scripture and devotion?

_____

_____

_____

WHAT DO YOU THINK?

How does it apply to your life?

_____

_____

_____

WHAT WILL YOU DO?

Don't just be a hearer of the word. Be a doer of the word. (James 1:22)

_____

_____

_____

NOW TALK TO GOD

This is where you turn your thoughts into prayer. It could be a prayer of gratitude or praise. It could be a prayer of confession or a request for God's help. It's up to you. Take a minute to write a prayer of response to what God said to you.

_____

_____

_____

_____

DAILY DEVOTIONS: DAY FORTY
SEIZE THE MOMENT!

"Be careful how you act; these are difficult days. Don't be fools; be wise: make the most of every opportunity you have for doing good."
EPHESIANS 5:15-16 (TLB)

Everyone has a dream, but most dreams never come true. It's not that we aren't smart enough, or outgoing enough, or even spiritual enough. Usually, our dreams don't come true because we're unwilling to take the necessary risks to reach them.

The Bible shares a sad one-sentence commentary about a king who failed to achieve an important ambition in his life: *"[King] Jehoshaphat built a fleet of trading ships to go to Ophir for gold, but they never set sail—they were wrecked at Ezion Geber"* (1 Kings 22:48 NIV).

While it's a tragedy for your ship to never come in, it's a greater tragedy to build a ship and never set sail. Imagine the energy and money expended by King Jehoshaphat. He built an entire fleet of ships to go after the gold, but not one of them set sail. Evidently a storm came up while they were in the harbor, and slammed the ships against the rocks. They were all destroyed.

Some people spend their whole lives waiting for their ship to come. But God isn't waiting for your ship to come in. He's waiting for you to sail your ship out of the harbor.

I know a man who for thirty years had a dream of starting a ministry, but he never took the risk to do anything about his dream. He never got his ship out of the harbor. Eventually, the man died—and so did his dream.

The Bible's antidote to that kind of tragic procrastination is as simple as an overdone catchphrase but excruciatingly difficult to apply at times: Just do it! The Bible says, *"Be careful how you act; these are difficult days. Don't be fools; be wise: make the most of every opportunity you have for doing good"* (Ephesians 5:15-16 TLB).

The Bible urges us to seize the moment and act now. To live a life with unfulfilled dreams is a tragedy. Ships aren't made for the harbor. They're made to set sail.

Are you ready to set sail?

WHAT DID YOU HEAR?

What did God say to you as you read today's Scripture and devotion?

_____

_____

_____

WHAT DO YOU THINK?

How does it apply to your life?

_____

_____

_____

WHAT WILL YOU DO?

Don't just be a hearer of the word. Be a doer of the word. (James 1:22)

_____

_____

_____

NOW TALK TO GOD

This is where you turn your thoughts into prayer. It could be a prayer of gratitude or praise. It could be a prayer of confession or a request for God's help. It's up to you. Take a minute to write a prayer of response to what God said to you.

_____

_____

_____

SMALL GROUP
RESOURCES

HELPS FOR HOSTS

Top Ten Ideas for New Hosts

CONGRATULATIONS! As the host of your small group, you have responded to the call to help shepherd Jesus' flock. Few other tasks in the family of God surpass the contribution you will be making. As you prepare to facilitate your group, whether it is one session or the entire series, here are a few thoughts to keep in mind.

Remember you are not alone. God knows everything about you, and he knew you would be asked to facilitate your group. Even though you may not feel ready, this is common for all good hosts. God promises, *"I will never leave you; I will never abandon you"* (Hebrews 13:5 TEV). Whether you are facilitating for one evening, several weeks, or a lifetime, you will be blessed as you serve.

1. **Don't try to do it alone.** Pray right now for God to help you build a healthy team. If you can enlist a co-host to help you shepherd the group, you will find your experience much richer. This is your chance to involve as many people as you can in building a healthy group. All you have to do is ask people to help. You'll be surprised at the response.

2. **Be friendly and be yourself.** God wants to use your unique gifts and temperament. Be sure to greet people at the door with a big smile . . . this can set the mood for the whole gathering. Remember, they are taking as big a step to show up at your house as you are to host a small group! Don't try to do things exactly like another host; do them in a way that fits you. Admit when you don't have an answer and apologize when you make a mistake. Your group will love you for it and you'll sleep better at night.

3. **Prepare for your meeting ahead of time.** Preview the session and write down your responses to each question.

4. **Pray for your group members by name.** Before your group arrives, take a few moments to pray for each member by name. You may want to review the *Small Group Prayer and Praise Report* at least once a week. Ask God to use your time together to touch the heart of each person in your group. Expect God to lead you to whomever he wants you to encourage or challenge in a special way. If you listen, God will surely lead.

5. **When you ask a question, be patient.** Someone will eventually respond. Sometimes people need a moment or two of silence to think

about the question. If silence doesn't bother you, it won't bother anyone else. After someone responds, affirm the response with a simple "thanks" or "great answer." Then ask, "How about somebody else?" or "Would someone who hasn't shared like to add anything?" Be sensitive to new people or reluctant members who aren't ready to say, pray, or do anything. If you give them a safe setting, they will blossom over time. If someone in your group is a wallflower who sits silently through every session, consider talking to them privately and encouraging them to participate. Let them know how important they are to you—that they are loved and appreciated, and that the group would value their input. Remember, still water often runs deep.

6. **Provide transitions between questions.** Ask if anyone would like to read the paragraph or Bible passage. Don't call on anyone, but ask for a volunteer, and then be patient until someone begins. Be sure to thank the person who reads aloud.

7. **Break into smaller groups occasionally.** With a greater opportunity to talk in a small circle, people will connect more with the study, apply more quickly what they're learning, and ultimately get more out of their small group experience. A small circle also encourages a quiet person to participate and tends to minimize the effects of a more vocal or dominant member.

8. **Small circles are also helpful during prayer time.** People who are unaccustomed to praying aloud will feel more comfortable trying it with just two or three others. Also, prayer requests won't take as much time, so circles will have more time to actually pray. When you gather back with the whole group, you can have one person from each circle briefly update everyone on the prayer requests from their subgroups. The other great aspect of subgrouping is that it fosters leadership development. As you ask people in the group to facilitate discussion or to lead a prayer circle, it gives them a small leadership step that can build their confidence.

9. **Rotate facilitators occasionally.** You may be perfectly capable of hosting each time, but you will help others grow in their faith and gifts if you give them opportunities to host the group.

10. **One final challenge (for new or first-time hosts).** Before your first opportunity to lead, look up each of the six passages listed below. Read each one as a devotional exercise to help prepare you with a shepherd's heart. Trust us on this one. If you do this, you will be more than ready for your first meeting.

"When Jesus saw the crowds, he had compassion on them, because they were harassed and helpless, like sheep without a shepherd. Then he said to his disciples, 'The harvest is plentiful but the workers are few. Ask the Lord of the harvest, therefore, to send out workers into his harvest field.'" MATTHEW 9:36–38 (NIV)

"I am the good shepherd; I know my sheep and my sheep know me—just as the Father knows me and I know the Father—and I lay down my life for the sheep." JOHN 10:14–15 (NIV)

"Be shepherds of God's flock that is under your care, serving as overseers—not because you must, but because you are willing, as God wants you to be; not greedy for money, but eager to serve; not lording it over those entrusted to you, but being examples to the flock. And when the Chief Shepherd appears, you will receive the crown of glory that will never fade away." 1 PETER 5:2–4 (NIV)

"If you have any encouragement from being united with Christ, if any comfort from his love, if any fellowship with the Spirit, if any tenderness and compassion, then make my joy complete by being like-minded, having the same love, being one in spirit and purpose. Do nothing out of selfish ambition or vain conceit, but in humility consider others better than yourselves. Each of you should look not only to your own interests, but also to the interests of others. Your attitude should be the same as that of Jesus Christ." PHILIPPIANS 2:1–5 (NIV)

"Let us hold unswervingly to the hope we profess, for he who promised is faithful. And let us consider how we may spur one another on toward love and good deeds. Let us not give up meeting together, as some are in the habit of doing, but let us encourage one another—and all the more as you see the Day approaching." HEBREWS 10:23–25 (NIV)

". . . but we were gentle among you, like a mother caring for her little children. We loved you so much that we were delighted to share with you not only the Gospel of God but our lives as well, because you had become so dear to us. . . . For you know that we dealt with each of you as a father deals with his own children, encouraging, comforting and urging you to live lives worthy of God, who calls you into his kingdom and glory." 1 THESSALONIANS 2:7–8, 11–12 (NIV)

FREQUENTLY ASKED QUESTIONS

HOW LONG WILL THIS GROUP MEET?

This study is six sessions long. We encourage your group to add a seventh session for a celebration. In your final session, each group member may decide if he or she desires to continue on for another study. At that time you may also want to do some informal evaluation, discuss your *Small Group Guidelines* (see page 148), and decide which study you want to do next. We recommend you visit our website at **www.rickwarren.org** for more video-based small-group studies.

WHO IS THE HOST?

The host is the person who coordinates and facilitates your group meetings. In addition to a host, we encourage you to select one or more group members to lead your group discussions. Several other responsibilities can be rotated, including refreshments, prayer requests, worship, or keeping up with those who miss a meeting. Shared ownership in the group helps everybody grow.

WHERE DO WE FIND NEW GROUP MEMBERS?

Recruiting new members can be a challenge for groups, especially new groups with just a few people, or existing groups that lose a few people along the way. We encourage you to use the *Circles of Life* diagram on page 150 of this study guide to brainstorm a list of people from your workplace, church, school, neighborhood, family, and so on. Then pray for the people on each member's list. Allow each member to invite several people from their list. Some groups fear that newcomers will interrupt the intimacy that members have built over time. However, groups that welcome newcomers generally gain strength with the infusion of new blood. Remember, the next person you add just might become a friend for eternity. Logistically, groups find different ways to add members. Some groups remain permanently open, while others choose to open periodically, such as at the beginning or end of a study. If your group becomes too large for easy, face-to-face conversations, you can subgroup, forming a second discussion group in another room.

HOW DO WE HANDLE THE CHILD-CARE NEEDS IN OUR GROUP?

Child-care needs must be handled very carefully. This is a sensitive issue. We suggest you seek creative solutions as a group. One common solution is to have the adults meet in the living room and share the cost of a baby sitter (or two) who can be with the kids in another part of the house. Another popular option is to have one home for the kids and a second home (close by) for the adults. If desired, the adults could rotate the responsibility of providing a lesson for the kids. This last option is great with school-age kids and can be a huge blessing to families.

SMALL GROUP GUIDELINES

It's a good idea for every group to put words to their shared values, expectations, and commitments. Such guidelines will help you avoid unspoken agendas and unmet expectations. We recommend you discuss your guidelines during Session 1 in order to lay the foundation for a healthy group experience. Feel free to modify anything that does not work for your group.

We agree to the following values:

Clear Purpose	To grow healthy spiritual lives by building a healthy small group community
Group Attendance	To give priority to the group meeting (call if I am absent or late)
Safe Environment	To create a safe place where people can be heard and feel loved (no quick answers, snap judgments, or simple fixes)
Be Confidential	To keep anything that is shared strictly confidential and within the group
Conflict Resolution	To avoid gossip and to immediately resolve any concerns by following the principles of Matthew 18:15–17
Spiritual Health	To give group members permission to speak into my life and help me live a healthy, balanced spiritual life that is pleasing to God
Limit Our Freedom	To limit our freedom by not serving or consuming alcohol during small group meetings or events so as to avoid causing a weaker brother or sister to stumble (1 Corinthians 8:1–13; Romans 14:19–21)
Welcome Newcomers	To invite friends who might benefit from this study and warmly welcome newcomers
Building Relationships	To get to know the other members of the group and pray for them regularly
Other	_____
	_____
	_____
	_____

We have also discussed and agree on the following items:

- Child Care _____

- Starting Time _____

- Ending Time _____

If you haven't already done so, take a few minutes to fill out the *Small Group Calendar* on page 152.

CIRCLES OF LIFE

SMALL GROUP CONNECTIONS

DISCOVER WHO YOU CAN CONNECT IN COMMUNITY

Use this chart to help carry out one of the values in the *Small Group Guidelines*, to "Welcome Newcomers."

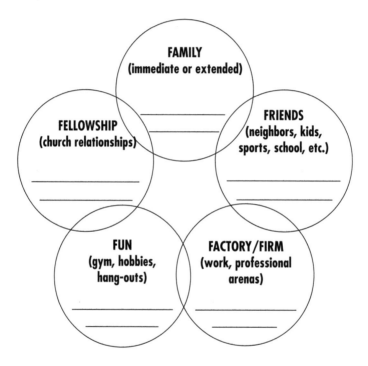

FOLLOW THIS SIMPLE THREE-STEP PROCESS:

1. List one to two people in each circle.

2. Prayerfully select one person or couple from your list and tell your group about them.

3. Give them a call and invite them to your next meeting. Over fifty percent of those invited to a small group say, "Yes!"

SMALL GROUP PRAYER AND PRAISE REPORT

This is a place where you can write each other's requests for prayer. You can also make a note when God answers a prayer. Pray for each other's requests. If you're new to group prayer, it's okay to pray silently or to pray by using just one sentence:

"God, please help _____ to _____."

DATE	PERSON	PRAYER REQUEST	PRAISE REPORT

SMALL GROUP CALENDAR

Healthy groups share responsibilities and group ownership. It might take some time for this to develop. Shared ownership ensures that responsibility for the group doesn't fall to one person. Use the calendar to keep track of social events, mission projects, birthdays, or days off. Complete this calendar at your first or second meeting. Planning ahead will increase attendance and shared ownership.

DATE	LESSON	LOCATION	FACILITATOR	SNACK OR MEAL
	Session 1			
	Session 2			
	Session 3			
	Session 4			
	Session 5			
	Session 6			

ANSWER KEY

SESSION ONE: BUILDING A LIFE OF FAITH

- Faith is **BELIEVING** when I don't see it.

- Faith is **OBEYING** when I don't understand it.

- Faith is **GIVING** when I don't have it.

- Faith is **PERSISTING** when I don't feel like it.

- Faith is **THANKING GOD** before I receive it.

- Faith is **TRUSTING** if I don't get it.

SESSION TWO: EXPECTING THE BEST

- When I expect the best it **HONORS** God.

- When I expect the best it **INCREASES** my ability.

- When I expect the best it **ENCOURAGES** others.

- **TUNE IN TO GOD** every morning.

- **THINK ON GOD'S PROMISES** throughout the day.

- **TRUST IN GOD'S LOVE** even when things look bad.

- **TALK WITH** other believers.

SESSION THREE: STRETCHING YOUR IMAGINATION

- You must let go of **DOUBT**.
  - **COMPARING** my abilities.
  - **REMEMBERING** my failures.
- Look for **A PROMISE**.
  - God promises **STRENGTH**.
  - God promises **SUCCESS**.
  - God promises **SUPPORT**.
- Lean on **THE LORD**.
- Launch out in **FAITH**.

SESSION FOUR: TAKING THE INITIATIVE

- Obey God **IMMEDIATELY**.

- Obey God **COMPLETELY**.

- Obey God **JOYFULLY**.

- Obey God **CONTINUALLY**.

SESSION FIVE: FACING YOUR FEARS

- The Principle of **INFORMATION**: Get the Facts.

- The Principle of **EVALUATION**: Count the Cost.

- The Principle of **PREPARATION**: Plan Your Steps.

- The Principle of **DECLARATION**: Announce Your Goal.

- The Principle of **INITIATION**: Let Go and Leap Out.

    - The Key to Daring Faith: **MOVE AGAINST YOUR FEAR**.

SESSION SIX: BELIEVING WHILE YOU'RE WAITING

- Phase One: **DREAM**

- Phase Two: **DECISION**

- Phase Three: **DELAY**

- Phase Four: **DIFFICULTY**

- Phase Five: **DEAD END**

- Phase Six: **DELIVERANCE**

- Remember **WHAT GOD CAN DO**.

- Rely on **GOD'S PROMISES**.

- Recognize **THE FACTS IN FAITH**.

- Rejoice **IN ANTICIPATION**.

- **CIRCUMSTANTIAL** deliverance.

- **PERSONAL** deliverance.

- **ULTIMATE** deliverance.